NARROW GAUGE STEAM LOCOMOTIVES
OF GREAT BRITAIN & IRELAND

C000021374

FIRST EDITION

The complete guide to all narrow gauge steam locomotives known to exist in Great Britain and Ireland of track gauges 1ft 6in to 4ft 6in

Peter Nicholson

Published by Platform 5 Publishing Ltd,
52 Broadfield Road, Sheffield S8 0XJ, England.

Printed in England by Berforts Information Press, Eynsham, Oxford.

ISBN 978 1 909431 11 9

© 2014 Platform 5 Publishing Ltd. All rights reserved. No part of this publication may be reproduced or transmitted in any form or by any means electronic, mechanical, photocopying, recording or otherwise, without prior permission of the publisher.

CONTENTS

Front Cover Photograph: A new classic railway scene: Bagnall 3023 of 1953, 0-4-2T "Isaac" approaches the Lynton & Barnstaple Railway's Woody Bay station with reconstructed L&BR coaches on 30 March 2014. **Peter Nicholson**

Left: Kerr Stuart 1049 of 1908, 2ft 6in gauge 'Brazil' class 0-4-2ST No. 2 "Excelsior" originally worked at Bowaters' paper mill in Sittingbourne. Now resident on the Great Whipsnade Railway, it heads a freight through the animal enclosure on 20 October 2007. **Cliff Thomas**

Back Cover Photograph (top): The Statfold Barn Railway is home to a variety of 2ft gauge locomotives. Waiting outside the shed on 15 September 2012 are Fowler 13355 of 1912, 0-4-2T "Saccharine" (left) and Peckett 2050 of 1944, 0-6-0ST "Harrogate". The Fowler locomotive saw active service in South Africa before being repatriated in 1979, whilst the Peckett is named after the gas works where it originally worked, then complete with a low-profile cab and lowered boiler fittings. **Peter Nicholson**

Back Cover Photograph (bottom): A typical locomotive builder's plate. **Peter Nicholson**

PREFACE TO THE FIRST EDITION

Welcome to the first edition of this new Platform 5 guide to narrow gauge steam locomotives resident in Great Britain and Ireland. It is hoped that this publication will fill the gap between the existing Platform 5 titles 'Preserved Locomotives of British Railways' which contains details of preserved standard gauge locomotives still in existence, and 'Miniature Railways of Great Britain and Ireland' which deals predominantly with locomotives of gauges from 7¼in to 18in.

The information contained in this book has been collated over many years of personal observation and correspondence since the mid-1960s, and including that made available through the Industrial Railway and Narrow Gauge Railway societies. The stock books and websites of the various railways also provide a very useful reference.

The locomotives are listed under builders' details in numerical order so that it can be easily seen how many of each type or builder exist in the UK and Ireland today. Other publications, also covering standard gauge locos, feature lists of the locos at the various railway locations, but this does not mean that a visit to those locations will result in all of them being available to see and photograph.

More often than not, some locos are hidden from view, dismantled in workshops or locked away in sheds. Also, locomotives often visit other railways these days on short-term gala visits or long-term hire, so will not be found within such lists although present at the time of the visit. Conversely they may be missing while away at another railway, all making such listings as to what is at the location somewhat misleading for the visitor. Locomotives not at publicly accessible locations will not be recorded at all, as they are here.

The purpose of this book is to place on record what is known to exist and where they are located. It should prove useful for all those wishing to see and photograph locomotives of any particular type or builder.

This is a constantly changing subject with historical details sometimes difficult to verify due to a lack of, or conflicting information published in the past. All entries have been very carefully checked, but inevitably some errors will have slipped through. Therefore the author would welcome notification of any corrections or updates to this book of which readers have first-hand knowledge. Of course, details of any narrow gauge steam locomotives currently in the British Isles and not included here, would be particularly welcome!

ACKNOWLEDGEMENTS & CONTACT DETAILS

Thanks are given to all those individuals and organisations who have assisted in the compiling of this book. A number of queries arose as the text was being finalised and I am grateful to those who have provide assistance at this stage, including Rob Gambrill, John Forshaw, Brian Gent, Phil Mason, Frank Saxby, Peter Smith and Cliff Thomas.

I would also like to thank those with whom I have travelled on "fact-finding" trips over the years, visiting the majority of the locations listed here at some time or other. In the now-distant past, it was with Rich Morris and the late Doug Semmens, but more recently with the Cardiff & Avonside Railway Society (CARS). Also, on many occasions over the past 30+ years, narrow gauge railways have been visited with my wife Pauline.

Grateful thanks are due to Cliff Thomas for supplying up-to-date digital images to fill in some of the important gaps in my own photo collection, where in many cases, I only had earlier, film prints or transparencies, at best.

Please send comments or amendments to the publisher's address on the title page, or by e-mail to updates@platform5.com.

This book is updated to include information received by 31 August 2014.

Peter Nicholson. August 2014.

▲ Avonside 1738 of 1915, 0-4-0T "Sezela No. 2", was formerly in use at the Sezela Sugar Mill, South Africa, until repatriated to the UK in 1972. It is now based on the Leighton Buzzard Railway, where it is seen on 26 May 2013. **Cliff Thomas**

▼ Avonside 2067 of 1933, 0-4-0T "Marchlyn", was sold from Penrhyn Slate Quarries to the USA in 1965, subsequently returning to the UK in 2011. It is pictured following restoration at its new home, the Statfold Barn Railway on 15 September 2012. **Peter Nicholson**

▲ Bagnall 1781 of 1905, 2-4-0T "Polar Bear" is seen at Amberley Museum on 13 July 2013, the day of its re-entry to service following overhaul. Originating from the old Groudle Glen Railway, Isle of Man, a replacement replica is being built for the present-day line, to be named "Brown Bear".

Cliff Thomas

▼ Bagnall 2135 of 1925, "Sir Tom", 0-4-0ST was built to operate at 3ft 6in gauge but has been regauged to 2ft in preservation, as has twin locomotive, Bagnall 2133 "Woto", with Alan Keef Ltd. "Sir Tom" is pictured at the spectacular Threlkeld Quarry & Mining Museum, near Keswick on 27 July 2013.

Cliff Thomas

INTRODUCTION

This book lists all narrow gauge steam locomotives known to exist in Great Britain and Ireland. These are of track gauges 1ft 6in to 4ft 6in, being those larger than miniature railways and less than standard gauge.

For the sake of completeness it includes those few locomotives that were built as steam but have subsequently been rebuilt with other means of propulsion, such as with a diesel engine. Similarly, there are few cases of non-steam locomotives rebuilt into steam, their original petrol or diesel engine replaced by a vertical boiler and steam engine unit.

All known steam locomotives, even if never available to view, are included, to provide a comprehensive record of those that are known to exist within the British Isles. The number of steam locos able to be included is considerably more than it would have been, just a few years ago. Not only have many been imported from countries around the world, of both British and overseas manufacture, but several new-build locos have been constructed. Details of further new-build projects currently under construction are given in Section 6.

Many of the locomotives brought in from abroad have been by private collectors, some of whom have decided to keep their acquisitions a closely guarded secret. This has resulted in a number of locomotives believed to be resident in the UK, although their actual or continued existence has not really been verified satisfactorily by independent observation. Unfortunately, they are in private hands on private lands and kept in secure accommodation with no public access ever allowed. They are mainly in 'as-arrived condition' it is believed, and have been so in some cases, for nearly 50 years. It would appear this situation is unlikely to change during the lifetime of the present owners.

A counter to this is Graham Lee, who has saved a great many locomotives from dereliction abroad, imported and restored them and regularly displays them to the public. This is not only on his own, amazing narrow gauge network, the Statfold Barn Railway on his farm in Staffordshire where he has also established a superb museum, but also allows these locos to appear elsewhere. This can be visiting a railway gala for the weekend or even helping out a railway suffering a motive power shortage. A somewhat different, and more welcome approach to saving historic locomotives for posterity.

Of those locomotives kept away from the enthusiast, it would be interesting to know which future edition of this book will be able to confirm their existence in the UK, and report they are now available to view and photograph, either on static display or even in operation. Hopefully (but perhaps somewhat optimistically), it will be compiled by the present author!

The number of narrow gauge steam locomotives that have been returned to operational condition and maintained by enthusiasts and commercial operators in recent years is quite remarkable. It is far in excess of anything that would have been thought possible back in the early 1960s when the number of steamable locos was at is nadir in this country. Many locos regularly visit other railways for gala events and so it is possible to see a dozen or more locomotives in steam at such occasions. We should all be grateful to those who have spent their money, time, effort and skills in making today's vibrant narrow gauge steam scene possible.

UPDATES

Updates to this book are published in Platform 5's monthly magazine, **Today's Railway UK,** which is the only magazine to carry a section dedicated to preserved locomotive stock changes. **Today's Railways UK** is available from good newsagents or on direct subscription (see inside back cover for further details).

GENERAL NOTES & LAYOUT OF INFORMATION

The book has been divided into six main sections to reflect the category of builder. Within each section locomotives are listed in alphabetical order of the builder's title. To ease reference, the builder's more commonly used, abbreviated name appears first, followed by the full title and address where the locomotives were constructed.

For example, locomotives by the Bagnall company appear immediately after Avonside, rather than listed under 'W', as they would be if using the full title of W. G. Bagnall Ltd.

Detailed notes relating to specific locomotives can be found at the end of each builder's entry, but the following details are consistent to each section:

BUILDER'S NO.

This is the number allocated to each locomotive by its manufacturer and is in effect the loco's 'pedigree'. It was usually displayed on the loco by means of a cast metal plate giving the builder's name and basic address with the year of completion/delivery of the loco.

Traditionally, this identity remains with the locomotive however much it is rebuilt subsequently, provided the original main frame is retained. However, there are a number of examples where locomotives continue to be identified by their builder's details although a new frame has been incorporated in a rebuild. The best known of which are Talyllyn Railway Nos 1 and 2. More recently this has occurred when a loco has undergone a through restoration, and is something likely to become more common in future. Where it is known the original main frame has been replaced this is mentioned in the loco's footnote.

Builder's Nos are often referred to as Works Nos. The latter term is really only applicable to the number given to a locomotive constructed in the workshops of a main line railway company. It was often displayed on a cast plate, similar in style to those produced by the commercial locomotive building companies. Examples were LNWR/LMSR Crewe, GNR/LNER Doncaster and GWR Swindon Works, among others, but in most cases this practice died out in later years.

YEAR

This is generally the year the locomotive was completed and delivered to the first customer. Where construction took place over several years, the beginning date is also quoted where known. e.g. Hudswell Clarke 1172 was started in 1915 but was set aside when the order was cancelled and not actually completed and delivered to another customer until 1924, hence 1915–24. This also applies to many of the present-day new-build locomotives.

Where the completion date is different to the year carried on the builder's plate this is noted.

TYPE

The Whyte notation is used with regard to locomotive wheel arrangements for those with coupled driving wheels. The number of leading wheels is given, followed by the number of driving wheels and then the trailing wheels.

Suffixes are used to denote locomotive types as follows:

T: Side Tank
PT: Pannier Tank
ST: Saddle Tank
WT: Well Tank
WTT: Well Tank and Side Tanks
IST: Inverted Saddle Tank
VB: Vertical Boiler
F: Fireless Locomotive
G: Geared Drive
+T: Tank Locomotive with a Tender

For locomotives where driving wheels are connected by means other than coupling rods, w is used to indicate powered axles.

CLASS

Manufacturers' class names are included where used by the builder and are known. Some class names quoted elsewhere were in fact telegraphic code words only. (Note, one Kerr Stuart 0-6-2T class has been quoted in the past as spelt Baretto, Barreto and Barretto!)

GAUGE

The track gauge covers locomotives from 1ft 6in to 4ft 6in. Most locomotives are of 600mm or 2ft gauge (nominal, see later), 2ft 6in or 3ft gauge. The question of '2ft gauge' is most complex and includes 600mm (Continental locomotives), 1ft 11½in, 1ft 11¾in and 2ft (610mm). As it is not always possible to know exactly what the precise gauge of any such locomotive is, in general they are given as the gauge by which the railway on which they operate is usually quoted. Therefore, Ffestiniog Railway locomotives are shown as 1ft 11½in gauge. The operational locos on the Vale of Rheidol are also this gauge, but many of the non-operational, museum display items are believed to be 2ft gauge. Brecon Mountain Railway is stated to be 1ft 11¾in gauge, so its locomotives are quoted likewise.

For operational purposes it is the 'back-to-back' measurement, on the inside of the wheel flanges that is the critical matter as this effects running through pointwork. Locomotives from Dinorwic and Penrhyn slate quarries were all of the lesser gauge of 1ft 10¾in. Most of these have now been regauged to 1ft 11½/2ft when restored for operation on heritage railways.

Where locomotives are known to have been regauged this is given in the loco's footnote.

LOCATION

This is where the locomotive is currently kept. Locations open to the public, at least once a year (e.g. Alan Keef Ltd), are detailed in the Appendix. The full address is given there (including Ordnance Survey grid reference) for the point of access to the location. Locomotives at private sites not accessible to the public are located only with the owner's name and nearest town and/or county.

The ownership of locomotives shown as P. Rampton and Vale of Rheidol Railway are as confirmed by the owners, to whom we are grateful for this clarification. It is expected the VoR Surrey locos will eventually be transferred to the new museum to be built at Aberystwyth, for public display. It is understood the P. Rampton-owned locos are likely to remain in Surrey. These locomotives are often shown elsewhere as being owned by the Phyllis Rampton Narrow Gauge Railway Trust, but in fact this trust does not own any locomotives.

RUNNING NO./NAME

In most cases these are as currently carried by the locomotive, but some are quoted in brackets to aid identification as they may be reinstated at a later date, such as following restoration after a lengthy period of dismantlement.

FOOTNOTES

These give basic details of the locomotive's origin, in the case of those acquired for preservation from industry in the British Isles this is the last such operator and/or location, with the date of entering preservation. In a few cases, locomotives originate from passenger railways, particularly Irish 3ft gauge examples.

Following withdrawal from use, engines often then passed through the hands of dealers or collectors and other preservation locations before reaching their present homes. Limited space prevents these from all being quoted.

For locomotives imported from abroad the country of origin only is given, along with the date when it was believed to have arrived in the UK. Other information in these notes includes regauging and rebuilding from one type or wheel arrangement to its present form.

ABBREVIATIONS

These are kept to the minimum to ease reading and understanding. However, the following have been used:

DFB: Deutscher Feldbahn (German Army Field Railway)
Lt Ry: Light Railway
NG: Narrow Gauge
RPS: Railway Preservation Society
RPSI: Railway Preservation Society of Ireland
WDLR: War Department Light Railways

PHOTOGRAPHS

These have been selected to show a good variety of locomotive builders and types, as well as different, present-day locations. They are all from within the period 2007 to 2014. It is of course impossible to depict an example of everything in the number of illustrations available, so apologies if a favourite has been omitted. All locos are 600mm/1ft 11½ in/2ft gauge unless stated.

▲ Bagnall 2820 of 1945, 4-4-0T "Isibutu" is one of 14 Bagnalls bought by Tongaat Sugar Co, South Africa. After working at various UK railways following repatriation, it is now at the Statfold Barn Railway. Photographed on 1 June 2013.   **Peter Nicholson**

PLATFORM 5 MAIL ORDER

PRESERVED LOCOMOTIVES
OF BRITISH RAILWAYS 16th edition

Fully updated edition of the complete guide to all former main line steam, diesel and electric locomotives and multiple units that are still in existence. It contains a complete list of all preserved main line locomotives and multiple units of BR and constituents. Fully revised and updated.

- All steam locomotives of British Railways, the 'Big Four' and their predecessors that are still in existence.
- Former war department locomotives, replica steam locos and new build steam locomotives.
- Detailed lists of diesel and electric locomotives, multiple units and railcars of BR and pre-nationalisation companies, incorporating extensive new additions and movements that have taken place in recent years.
- Technical information for steam locomotives, with BR power classifications now included for all ex-BR, 'Big Four' and WD locomotives.
- Currently carried number, former numbers, nameplates, build dates, builder and home locations for every locomotive and multiple unit.
- A comprehensive list of preservation sites and operating railways with OS grid references.
- Over 90 colour illustrations.

PRESERVED LOCOMOTIVES OF BRITISH RAILWAYS

ROBERT PRITCHARD & PETER HALL

STEAM, DIESEL & ELECTRIC LOCOMOTIVES & MULTIPLE UNITS

Compiled by Today's Railways UK writers, Robert Pritchard and Peter Hall, Preserved Locomotives 16th edition is the most comprehensive guide of its nature available. Published 2014. A5 size. 160 pages. **£16.95**

HOW TO ORDER

Telephone your order and credit/debit card details to our 24-hour sales orderline:
0114 255 8000 or Fax: 0114 255 2471. An answerphone is attached for calls made outside of normal UK office hours. Or send your credit/debit card details, sterling cheque, money order or British Postal order payable to 'Platform 5 Publishing Ltd.' to:

**Mail Order Department (NGSL), Platform 5 Publishing Ltd,
52 Broadfield Road, SHEFFIELD, S8 0XJ, ENGLAND.**
Please add postage & packing: 10% UK; 20% Europe; 30% Rest of World. Please allow 28 days for delivery in the UK.

1. BRITISH COMMERCIAL LOCOMOTIVE BUILDERS

ATKINSON WALKER

Atkinson Walker Wagons Ltd, Frenchwood Works, Preston, Lancashire.

Builder's No.	Year	Type	Class	Gauge	Location	Running No./ Name	Notes
114	1928	(4wTVB)	A3	3ft	Ulster Folk & Transport Museum	11 *Phoenix*	1

1. New to Clogher Valley Railway; sold to County Donegal Railways. Rebuilt with a diesel engine at Dundalk in 1932. Withdrawn 12/1959.

AVELING & PORTER

Aveling & Porter Ltd, Rochester, Kent.

Builder's No.	Year	Type	Class	Gauge	Location	Running No./ Name	Notes
1607	1880	2-2-0WT	5nhp	3ft	Hollycombe Steam Museum	(*Excelsior*)	1

1. Used by James Whittaker & Son, Scout Moor Quarries, Ramsbottom, Lancashire until 1910. Acquired for preservation as a static exhibit by Aveling Barford Ltd in 1961; to Hollycombe in 1984.

AVONSIDE

The Avonside Engine Co. Ltd, Filwood Road, Fishponds, Bristol.

Builder's No.	Year	Type	Class	Gauge	Location	Running No./ Name	Notes
1547	1908	0-6-0T		3ft	Alan Keef Ltd, Ross-on-Wye	*Nancy*	1
1720	1915	0-4-0T		2ft	N. Williams, Reading	2 *Sezela No. 2*	2
1738	1915	0-4-0T		2ft	Leighton Buzzard Railway	*Sezela No. 4*	2
1748	1916	0-4-0T	Charlton	1ft 6in	Crossness Pumping Station	No.1 *Woolwich*	3
1928	1923	0-4-0T		2ft	N. Williams, Reading	6 *Sezela No. 6*	2
2057	1931	0-4-4-0T		2ft 0½in	P. Rampton, Surrey	*Renishaw 4*	4
2066	1933	0-4-0T		1ft 10¾in	Beamish	*Ogwen*	5
2067	1933	0-4-0T		2ft	Statfold Barn Railway	*Marchlyn*	6
2071	1933	0-4-0T		2ft	Leighton Buzzard Railway	*Elidir*	7

1. Staveley Minerals Ltd, Eastwell Quarries, Leicestershire until 10/1961. Stored for Irish Narrow Gauge Trust, Dromod, awaiting completion of restoration.
2. Repatriated from South Africa – 1738 in 1972.
3. New to Royal Arsenal Railways, Woolwich; at Bicton Woodland Railway, 1962-10/2000. Under restoration and not yet on public display.
4. Repatriated from South Africa 1969.
5. Penrhyn Slate Quarries, Bethesda until 7/1965 (regauged from 2ft); repatriated from USA 5/2012. To be regauged back to 2ft.
6. Penrhyn Slate Quarries, Bethesda until 7/1965 (where regauged to 1ft 10¾in); repatriated from USA 5/2011.
7. Dinorwic Slate Quarries, Llanberis until 7/1966 (where regauged to 1ft 10¾in); repatriated from Canada 5/2006.

▲ Bagnall 3023 of 1953, 0-4-2T "Isaac" is one of four such locomotives supplied to Rustenberg Platinum Mine, South Africa. Now privately-owned, it arrived for use on the Lynton & Barnstaple Railway on 29 November 2013. Loco builder and restorer, John Uphill, stands alongside "Isaac" at Woody Bay station on 30 March 2014. **Peter Nicholson**

▼ Baguley 2007 of 1921, 0-4-0T "Rishra" was repatriated by the late Mike Satow on his retirement from working in India. Now based on the Leighton Buzzard Railway, "Rishra" has visited several other railways, including the Devon Railway Centre, where it is seen on 14 August 2011 double-heading with Kerr Stuart 3114, itself on loan to the DRC that season from the Vale of Rheidol Railway. **Peter Nicholson**

▲ Barclay 1578 of 1918, 0-6-0T "Gertrude" had a protracted restoration that was completed in 2009. Restored by and on lease to Exmoor Transport, it is based on the Welsh Highland Heritage Railway, but was visiting the Statfold Barn Railway on 27 March 2010. **Peter Nicholson**

▼ Barclay 1871 of 1925, 0-4-0T "Jack" is of unusual appearance as it worked on the restricted-height lines within Granton Gasworks, Edinburgh, and has front or 'wing' tanks. Owned by Nick Williams, it visits railway gala events, such as the Devon Railway Centre's on 19 August 2012. **Peter Nicholson**

BAGNALL

W. G. Bagnall Ltd, Castle Engine Works, Stafford, Staffordshire. (See also Section 5 Scale Model Locomotives).

Builder's No.	Year	Type	Class	Gauge	Location	Running No./ Name	Notes
1278	1890	(0-4-0IST)		2ft	Welsh Highland Heritage Railway	*The Coalition*	1
1445	1895	(0-4-0ST)		2ft	Welsh Highland Heritage Railway	*The Eclipse*	1
1484	1896	2-4-0T		2ft	Groudle Glen Railway	*Sea Lion*	2
1491	1897	0-4-0ST		2ft	Amerton Railway	*Isabel*	3
1568	1899	0-4-0ST		2ft	W. Daken, Sandbach	*Dorothy*	4
1760	1906	0-4-0ST		2ft	West Lancashire Light Railway	*Sybil*	5
1781	1905	2-4-0T		2ft	Amberley Museum	*Polar Bear*	6
1889	1911	0-4-0ST	Mercedes	3ft	Amerton Railway	No. 1	7
2029	1916	2-6-2T		2ft 6in	Vale of Rheidol Railway, Surrey	AK16	8
2043	1917	0-4-0ST		1ft 11½in	Yaxham Light Railways	*Kidbrooke*	9
2067	1918	0-4-0ST		2ft	Amberley Museum	*Peter*	10
2087	1919	0-4-0ST		2ft	Abbey Pumping Station, Leicester	*Leonard*	11
2088	1919	0-4-0ST		2ft	Bredgar & Wormshill Lt Railway	No. 4 *Armistice*	11
2090	1919	0-4-0ST		2ft	R. Gambrill, Hampshire	*Pixie*	12
2091	1919	0-4-0ST		2ft	Bursledon Light Railway	*Wendy*	13
2133	1924	0-4-0ST		2ft	Alan Keef Ltd	*Woto*	14
2135	1925	0-4-0ST		2ft	Threlkeld Quarry	*Sir Tom*	14
2192	1922	0-6-2T		2ft 6in	Vale of Rheidol Railway, Surrey	No. 3 *Conqueror*	15
2216	1923	2-4-0F		2ft 6in	Sittingbourne & Kemsley Lt Ry	*Unique*	16
2228	1924	0-4-4T		2ft	Vale of Rheidol Ry, Aberystwyth	18BG	17
2287	1926	4-4-0T		1ft 11½in	G. Walton-Binns, Middlesbrough	*Sinembe*	18
2457	1932	4-6-2		2ft	Vale of Rheidol Railway, Surrey	38	19
2460	1932	4-6-2		2ft	Vale of Rheidol Railway, Surrey	41	19
2472	1932	0-6-2T	Baretto	2ft 6in	Sittingbourne & Kemsley Lt Ry	*Alpha*	15
2511	1934	0-6-2T	Baretto	2ft 6in	Sittingbourne & Kemsley Lt Ry	*Triumph*	15
2545	1936	0-4-4-0T		600mm	P. Rampton, Surrey	*Renishaw 5*	20
2624	1940	0-6-2T	Baretto	2ft 6in	Sittingbourne & Kemsley Lt Ry	*Superb*	15
2627	1940	4-4-0T		1ft 11½in	G. Walton-Binns, Middlesbrough	*A. Boulle*	21
2819	1946	4-4-0T		1ft 11½in	Lynton & Barnstaple Railway	*Charles Wytock*	18
2820	1945	4-4-0T		2ft	Statfold Barn Railway	*Isibutu*	22
2895	1948	0-4-2T		2ft	P. Rampton, Surrey		23
3023	1953	0-4-2T		2ft	Lynton & Barnstaple Railway	*Isaac*	24
3024	1953	0-4-4-0T		2ft 6in	Welshpool & Llanfair Lt Ry	No. 6 *Monarch*	25
3050	1953	0-4-2T		2ft	Welsh Highland Heritage Railway	*Gelert*	24

1. Rebuilt by J. W. Greaves & Sons, Llechwedd Slate Quarry, Blaenau Ffestiniog as overhead wire electric locomotives in 1930 and 1927 respectively.
2. Groudle Glen Railway until 1967, then at various locations in England and the Isle of Man until returned to the new GGR 9/1987.
3. Cliffe Hill Granite Co. Ltd, Markfield, Leicestershire until 3/1953.
4. J. W Greaves & Sons, Llechwedd Slate Quarry, Blaenau Ffestiniog until 12/1972. Dismantled to frame and cab for conversion to electric loco c1930, but never completed.
5. Dinorwic Slate Quarries, Llanberis until 1/1969. Regauged from 1ft 10¾in.
6. Groudle Glen Railway, Isle of Man until 6/1967.
7. British Railways, Beeston Sleeper Depot 7/1956 -1962; Departmental No. ED10. Previously Judkins Ltd, Tuttle Hill Granite Quarry, Nuneaton.
8. Repatriated from India 1/1997.
9. Oakeley Slate Quarries Co. Ltd, Blaenau Ffestiniog until 1961.
10. Cliffe Hill Granite Co. Ltd, Markfield, Leicestershire until 8/1965.
11. Birmingham, Tame & Rea District Drainage Board, Minworth until 4/1961.
12. Staveley Minerals Ltd, Cranford Quarries, Northants until 5/1962; Cadeby Light Railway (Rev. E. R. Boston), until 2005.

13. Dorothea Slate Quarry Co. Ltd, Nantlle until 1962.
14. British Insulated Callender's Cables Ltd, Belvedere until 1969. Regauged from 3ft 6in.
15. Bowaters UK Pulp & Paper Mills Ltd, Sittingbourne until 10/1969.
16. Bowaters UK Pulp & Paper Mills Ltd, Sittingbourne until 10/1969. The only surviving narrow gauge fireless locomotive in the UK.
17. Repatriated from Hong Kong 9/2007.
18. Repatriated from South Africa 4/1994. Restoration of 2287 nearing completion and new home sought.
19. Repatriated from India c1994.
20. Repatriated from South Africa 1969.
21. Repatriated from South Africa. Restoration nearing completion and new home sought.
22. Repatriated from South Africa 1972.
23. Repatriated from South Africa 1976
24. Repatriated from South Africa 4/1982
25. Bowaters UK Pulp & Paper Mills Ltd, Sittingbourne until 6/1966.

BAGULEY

E. E. Baguley Ltd, Burton-on-Trent, Staffordshire.

Builder's No.	Year	Type	Class	Gauge	Location	Running No./ Name	Notes
2007	1921	0-4-0T		2ft	Leighton Buzzard Railway	No. 3 *Rishra*	1

1. Repatriated from India 1971.

▲ Barclay 2264 of 1949 is one of three 3ft gauge 0-4-0WTs delivered to Bord na Mona, Ireland. Barclay 2263 was rebuilt as Talyllyn Railway No. 7 "Tom Rolt", but BnM No. LM44 has been restored to original condition by the Irish Steam Preservation Society for its line at Stradbally, Co. Laois, as seen on 24 April 2011. **Peter Nicholson**

BARCLAY

Andrew Barclay Sons & Co. Ltd, Caledonia Works, Kilmarnock, Ayrshire.

Builder's No.	Year	Type	Class	Gauge	Location	Running No./ Name	Notes
840	1899	0-4-0T	Class A	3ft	Scottish RPS, Bo'ness	(*Fair Maid of Foyers*)	1
984	1903	0-4-0ST	Class D	2ft	Hampton & Kempton Water Works Railway	3 *Darent*	2
988	1903	0-4-0T	Class D	2ft	Beamish	5 *Esme*	3
1431	1918	0-4-0WT	Class E	2ft 3in	Talyllyn Railway	No. 6 *Douglas*	4
1578	1918	0-6-0T	Class L	600mm	Welsh Highland Heritage Railway	*Gertrude*	5
1641	1919	0-6-0T	Class L	2ft	Leighton Buzzard Railway	*Doll*	5
1871	1925	0-4-0T	Class D	2ft	N. Williams, Reading	9 *Jack*	6
1994	1931	0-4-0WT	Class E	2ft	Beamish	*Glyder*	7
1995	1931	0-4-0WT	Class E	2ft	Hollycombe Steam Museum	70 *Caledonia*	8
2207	1946	0-4-0T	Class D	2ft 6in	Welshpool & Llanfair Lt Ry	*Dougal*	9
2263	1949	0-4-2T	Mod. E	2ft 3in	Talyllyn Railway	No. 7 *Tom Rolt*	10
2264	1949	0-4-0WT	Mod. E	3ft	Irish Steam Preservation Society	No. 2 LM44	11
2265	1949	0-4-0WT	Mod. E	3ft	Giants Causeway & Bushmills Ry	No. 3 *Shane*	11

1. British Aluminium Co. Ltd, Foyers Works, Loch Ness until 1964.
2. Scottish Gas Board, Provan Gasworks, Glasgow until 1961. Rebuilt as 0-4-0ST from 0-4-0 front tank in 2003 and regauged from 2ft 6in, by the Provan Group, Kent.
3. Scottish Gas Board, Granton Gasworks, Edinburgh until 5/1960. Owned by National Museum of Scotland; to Beamish 1/13 for three-year loan.
4. RAF Calshot, Hampshire until 1949. Regauged from 1ft 11½in and presented to TR in 1953. Sometimes carries the name *Duncan*.
5. Stewarts & Lloyds Ltd, Bilston, Staffordshire until 11/1960; 1578 regauged from 2ft in 2006.
6. Scottish Gas Board, Granton Gasworks, Edinburgh until 1968.
7. Penrhyn Slate Quarries, Bethesda until 7/1965(where regauged to1ft 10¾in); repatriated from USA 5/2012.
8. Dinorwic Slate Quarries, Llanberis until 8/1962(where regauged to 1ft 10¾in).
9. Scottish Gas Board, Provan Gasworks, Glasgow until 4/1962. Also carries identity *G.C.G.D Provan Works No. 1*.
10. Bord na Mona, Clonsast, Co Offaly, Ireland until 3/1969. Originally a 3ft gauge 0-4-0WT, major components including boiler, wheels and cylinders used in a new-build locomotive completed by Talyllyn Railway in 1991 – as detailed in Section 3. The fate of the main frame not known.
11. Bord na Mona, Clonsast, Co. Offaly until 1969.

BELLIS & SEEKINGS

Bellis & Seekings Ltd, Ledsam Street, Birmingham.

Builder's No.	Year	Type	Class	Gauge	Location	Running No./ Name	Notes
-	1874	0-6-0WT		2ft 8in	Swanage Railway, Corfe Castle	(*Secundus*)	1

1. Pike Bros, Fayle & Co. Ltd, Furzebrook, Dorset until 1955.

BEYER PEACOCK

Beyer Peacock & Co. Ltd, Gorton, Manchester.

Builder's No.	Year	Type	Class	Gauge	Location	Running No./ Name	Notes
1253	1873	2-4-0T		3ft	Isle of Man Steam Railway	No. 1 *Sutherland*	
1255	1873	2-4-0T		3ft	Museum of Science & Industry	No. 3 *Pender*	1
1416	1874	2-4-0T		3ft	Isle of Man Steam Railway	No. 4 *Loch*	
1417	1874	2-4-0T		3ft	Isle of Man Steam Railway	No. 5 *(Mona)*	
1524	1875	2-4-0T		3ft	Port Erin Railway Museum	No. 6 *Peveril*	
2028	1880	2-4-0T		3ft	J. Edwards, Isle of Man	No. 14 *Thornhill*	2
2038	1880	2-4-0T		3ft	Southwold Railway Project	No. 7 *Tynwald*	3
2817	1887	0-4-0WT		1ft 6in	Narrow Gauge Railway Museum	*Dot*	4
2825	1887	0-4-0ST+T		1ft 6in	National Railway Museum, York	*Wren*	5
3496	1902	0-6-0T		2ft 6in	Welshpool & Llanfair Lt Ry	822 *The Earl*	
3497	1902	0-6-0T		2ft 6in	Welshpool & Llanfair Lt Ry	823 *Countess*	
3610	1894	2-4-0T		3ft	Isle of Man Steam Railway	No. 8 *(Fenella)*	
3815	1896	2-4-0T		3ft	Port Erin Railway Museum	No. 9 *Douglas*	
4662	1905	2-4-0T		3ft	Isle of Man Steam Railway	No. 10 *G. H. Wood*	
4663	1905	2-4-0T		3ft	Isle of Man Steam Railway	No. 11 *Maitland*	
5126	1908	2-4-0T		3ft	Isle of Man Steam Railway	No. 12 *Hutchinson*	
5292	1909	0-4-0+0-4-0		1ft 11½in	Welsh Highland Railway	No. 1K No. 2K	6
5382	1910	2-4-0T		3ft	Isle of Man Steam Railway	No. 13 *Kissack*	
6296	1926	2-4-0T		3ft	Port Erin Railway Museum	16 *Mannin*	
6639	1930	4-8-2+2-8-4	GL	3ft 6in	Museum of Science & Industry	2352	7
6919	1939	2-6-2+2-6-2	NG/G16	2ft	Welsh Highland Railway	109	8
6925	1937	2-6-2+2-6-2	NG/G16	2ft	Exmoor Steam Railway	115	9
7431	1951	2-6-2+2-6-2	NG/G16	2ft	Exmoor Steam Railway	130	9
7827	1957	4-8-2+2-8-4		3ft 6in	Summerlee	4112 *(Springbok)*	10
7863	1958	2-6-2+2-6-2	NG/G16	1ft 11½in	Welsh Highland Railway	138 *Millennium/ Mileniwm*	11
7865	1958	2-6-2+2-6-2	NG/G16	1ft 11½in	Welsh Highland Railway	140	12
7868	1958	2-6-2+2-6-2	NG/G16	1ft 11½in	Welsh Highland Railway	143	11

1. Isle of Man Railway until c1981. Sectionalised and displayed at MOSI Manchester with wheels turned by electric motor.
2. Manx Northern Railway until 4/1905; Isle of Man Railway until 1979.
3. Isle of Man Railway until dismantled remains moved to England 2012.
4. Beyer Peacock & Co. Ltd, Gorton Foundry, Manchester until 6/1961.
5. British Railways Horwich Works until 1964.
6. Repatriated from Tasmania in 1947 by Beyer Peacock; to Festiniog Railway 3/1966. First Beyer Garratt built.
7. Repatriated from South Africa c1984.
8. Repatriated from South Africa 1995.
9. Repatriated from South Africa 1/1998.
10. Built by North British as subcontractor – builder's No. 27770. See North British.
11. Repatriated from South Africa 1/1997. SAR No.143 was the last Garratt built by Beyer Peacock.
12. Repatriated from South Africa 4/1997.

▲ Bellis & Seekings 2ft 8in gauge 0-6-0WT, built in 1874 is claimed to be the only full-size steam locomotive to be built in Birmingham in the UK. Originally employed at Pike Bros, Fayle & Co. Ltd, Furzebrook, Dorset, the loco was preserved by the Birmingham Locomotive Club in 1955, and is now on display in the Swanage Railway museum at Corfe Castle station, as seen on 9 May 2014.
Peter Nicholson

▼ Beyer Peacock 3496 of 1902, 2ft 6in gauge 0-6-0T No. 822 "The Earl" and Beyer Peacock 3497 No. 823 "Countess" are the original Welshpool & Llanfair Light Railway locomotives, later passing into the ownership of the GWR and subsequently British Railways. No. 822 arrives at Llanfair Caereinion on 22 August 2009.
Peter Nicholson

▲ Beyer Peacock 4662 of 1905, 2-4-0T No. 10 "G. H Wood" is one of 14 locomotives built by the Manchester company for the Isle of Man Railway. All but one survive, although not all are complete or remain on the island. No. 10 is seen at Port Erin on 31 July 2009, restored in the green livery from the Marquis of Ailsa-operated period, 1967-1971. **Peter Nicholson**

▼ De Winton "Chaloner" is one of no fewer than eight surviving examples of the vertical boiler locomotives built in Caernarfon in the late 1800s for the local slate industry. Restored and maintained in working order by Alfred and David Fisher, it is based on the Leighton Buzzard Railway but visits other railways. It is seen at Alan Keef's annual open day on 25 September 2010. **Cliff Thomas**

BLACK HAWTHORN

Black, Hawthorn & Co. Ltd, Gateshead.

Builder's No.	Year	Type	Class	Gauge	Location	Running No./ Name	Notes
748	1883	0-4-0T		600mm	Tanfield Railway	11 *Escucha*	1
859	1885	0-4-0ST		3ft	National Trust, Penrhyn Castle	*Kettering Furnaces No. 3*	2

1. Repatriated from Spain 4/1984. Built as a 640mm gauge 0-4-0ST. Dismantled, with main frame kept in a locked shed.
2. Kettering Iron & Coal Co. Ltd, Kettering until 1963.

DE WINTON

De Winton & Co., Union Works, Caernarvon.

Builder's No.	Year	Type	Class	Gauge	Location	Running No./ Name	Notes
-	1877	0-4-0TVB		2ft	Leighton Buzzard Railway	*Chaloner*	1
-	1877	0-4-0TVB		1ft 10¾in	Rampton, Capel Bangor	*Kathleen*	2
-	1877	0-4-0TVB		1ft 10¾ in	Narrow Gauge Railway Museum	*George Henry*	3
-	1878	0-4-0TVB		3ft	Hanson Aggregates, Penmaenmawr	(*Penmaen*)	4
-	1893	0-4-0TVB		3ft	National Trust, Penrhyn Castle	(*Watkin*)	5
-	1893	0-4-0TVB		1ft 11½in	R. Gambrill, Hampshire	(*Gelli*)	6
-	1894	0-4-0TVB		1ft 11½in	Brecon Mountain Railway	*Pendyffryn*	7
-	1895	0-4-0TVB		3ft	Welsh Highland Railway, Dinas	*Llanfair*	5

1. Pen-yr-Orsedd Slate Quarry, Nantlle until 9/1960. Maintained in working order.
2. Penrhyn Slate Quarries, Bethesda until 1/1966.
3. Penrhyn Slate Quarries, Bethesda until 5/1956.
4. Dismantled remains lie on Level 2, Bottom Bank East Quarry, Penmaenmawr granite quarries.
5. Kingston Minerals Ltd, Penmaenmawr until 2/1966.
6. Pen-yr-Orsedd Slate Quarry, Nantlle where dismantled in 1949, but the main frame survived in use as the edge to a pit in the loco shed until discovered in 1991. Now being rebuilt as parts become available.
7. Pen-yr-Orsedd Slate Quarry, Nantlle until 5/1965. New main frame built by A. J. Hills, Knowle, Warwickshire c1969 and original scrapped.

DÜBS

Dübs & Co. Ltd, Glasgow Locomotive Works, Glasgow.

Builder's No.	Year	Type	Class	Gauge	Location	Running No./ Name	Notes
2178	1885	0-6-0T		3ft	Isle of Man Steam Railway	15 *Caledonia*	1
2890	1892	0-6-2T	Class IN1 5C	3ft	West Clare Railway	5C *Slieve Callan*	2
3819	1899	4-8-2T	Class A	3ft 6in	Mizens Railway		3

1. Manx Northern Railway until 4/1905.
2. CIE (West Clare Section) until 1959, then stored at Inchicore Works, Dublin until 10/1961.
3. Repatriated from South Africa 5/2011. On static display at the entrance to this 7¼in gauge railway.

ENGLAND

George England & Co. Ltd, Hatcham Iron Works, Pomeroy Street, New Cross, London.

Builder's No.	Year	Type	Class	Gauge	Location	Running No./ Name	Notes
200	1863	0-4-0ST+T	Small England	1ft 11½in	Ffestiniog Railway	No. 1 *Princess*	1
-	1863	0-4-0ST+T	Small England	1ft 11½in	Ffestiniog Railway	No. 2 *Prince*	2
-	1864	0-4-0ST+T	Small England	1ft 11½in	Ffestiniog Railway	*Palmerston*	3
234	1867	0-4-0ST+T	Large England	1ft 11½in	Ffestiniog Railway	No. 5 *Welsh Pony/ Merlen Gymreig*	4

1. Built as 0-4-0T; tender fitted by 1880; rebuilt as a saddle tank 1893-95. Restored cosmetically; to be kept as a static exhibit to preserve originality.
2. Built as 0-4-0T. Claimed to be the oldest working narrow gauge loco in the world.
3. Built as 0-4-0T.
4. Restoration to working order in progress.

FALCON

Falcon Engine & Car Works, Loughborough, Leicestershire.

Builder's No.	Year	Type	Class	Gauge	Location	Running No./ Name	Notes
265	1897	4-4-0	F4	2ft	Vale of Rheidol Railway, Surrey	SSE 1912	1
266	1897	4-4-0	F4	2ft	Vale of Rheidol Railway, Surrey	*Lisboa*	1

1. Repatriated from Mozambique 8/1999. Ex-Beira Railway Nos 27 and 28 respectively.

FLETCHER JENNINGS

Fletcher Jennings & Co. Ltd, Lowca Engine Works, Whitehaven, Cumberland.

Builder's No.	Year	Type	Class	Gauge	Location	Running No./ Name	Notes
42	1864	0-4-2ST	C	2ft 3in	Talyllyn Railway	No. 1 *Talyllyn*	1
63	1866	0-4-0WT	B.b.	2ft 3in	Talyllyn Railway	No. 2 *Dolgoch*	2
172L	1880	0-4-0T	E	3ft 2¼in	Amberley Museum	1 *Townsend Hook*	3
173L	1880	0-4-0T	E	3ft 2¼in	Beamish	5 *William Finlay*	3

1. Date usually given as 1865 but locomotive was completed on 24/9/1864. Rebuilt from 0-4-0ST 1867. Few, if any original parts retained in various rebuilds. Rebuilt TR c1900 with new main frame supplied by Bagnall. Sometimes carries the name *Skarloey*
2. Rebuilt by Gibbons Bros Ltd, Brierley Hill, Staffordshire in 1963 with new main frame and Hunslet boiler. Sometimes carries the name *Rheneas*.
3. Dorking Greystone Lime Co., Betchworth, Surrey until 4/1960.

▲ Dübs 2890 of 1892, No. 5C "Slieve Callan", 3ft gauge 0-6-2T, ex-West Clare Railway was on static display at Ennis station, Co, Clare for many years. Now restored, it works on a short, re-opened section of the WCR at Moyasta, where seen on 23 April 2011. **Peter Nicholson**

▼ England 0-4-0ST+T of 1864 "Palmerston" is one four surviving examples of the early narrow gauge steam locomotives built in London for the Festiniog Railway. "Palmerston", restored from derelict condition, visited Hollycombe Working Steam Museum, West Sussex on 31 May 2008. **Peter Nicholson**

▲ Fletcher Jennings 63 of 1866, 2ft 3in gauge 0-4-0WT "Dolgoch" has been Talyllyn Railway No. 2 all its life, although little of the original remains, other than its general appearance. It is seen in Quarry Sidings on 5 May 2013 at the opening of The Guest House covered storage facility named in honour of Phil Guest (1944-2008), a long-standing TR driver and supporter. **Cliff Thomas**

▼ Fowler 18800 of 1930, 0-6-0WT "Limpopo" was one of a large number of locomotives imported from Mozambique in 1998/99, which filled many gaps in the coverage of loco types in the UK. Beautifully restored by the Bredgar & Wormshill Railway in Kent, it is seen on 8 April 2007. **Cliff Thomas**

FOWLER

John Fowler & Co. (Leeds) Ltd, Hunslet, Leeds.

Builder's No.	Year	Type	Class	Gauge	Location	Running No./ Name	Notes
10249	1905	0-6-0T+T		600mm	Vale of Rheidol Railway		1
11938	1909	0-4-2T		600mm	Vale of Rheidol Railway	21	2
13355	1912	0-4-2T		2ft	Statfold Barn Railway	*Saccharine*	3
13573	1912	0-4-2T		2ft	Bredgar & Wormshill Lt Ry	10 *Zambezi*	4
15513	1920	0-4-2T		600mm	West Lancashire Light Railway	48	2
15515	1920	0-6-2T		600mm	Vale of Rheidol Railway	23	2
15991	1923	0-6-0WT		2ft	West Lancashire Light Railway	3 *Cheetal*	5
18800	1930	0-6-0WT		2ft	Bredgar & Wormshill Lt Ry	9 *Limpopo*	2

1. Possibly Fowler 9465; repatriated from USA 11/1998.
2. Repatriated from Mozambique 10/1998.
3. Repatriated from South Africa 4/1979.
4. Repatriated from Mozambique 8/1999; regauged from 500mm.
5. Repatriated from India 1985. On loan from Leeds Museums & Galleries.

GARTELL

Gartell Light Railway, Common Lane, Yenston, near Templecombe, Somerset (See also Section 3. Locomotives built by owners and operators).

Builder's No.	Year	Type	Class	Gauge	Location	Running No./ Name	Notes
-	2006	0-6-0WTT		2ft	Lynton & Barnstaple Railway	*Axe*	1

1. A rebuild of 600mm gauge Kerr Stuart 2451 of 1915, including replacement frame and boiler etc. Work carried out by John Uphill in Gartell's workshops under contract.

GKN SANKEY

GKN Sankey Ltd, Castle Works, Hadley, Telford, Shropshire.

Builder's No.	Year	Type	Class	Gauge	Location	Running No./ Name	Notes
-	1990	4wG		3ft	Ironbridge Gorge Museum		1

1. Working replica of Trevithick locomotive with flangeless wheels; runs on plateway-type flanged rails.

GREAT NORTHERN STEAM

Great Northern Steam Co. Ltd, Unit 3, Forge Way, Cleveland Industrial Estate, Darlington, County Durham.

Builder's No.	Year	Type	Class	Gauge	Location	Running No./ Name	Notes
20	2004	0-4-0WT		1ft 7in	Great Laxey Mine Railway	*Ant*	1
21	2004	0-4-0WT		1ft 7 in	Great Laxey Mine Railway	*Bee*	2

1. Replica of original Great Laxey Mine locomotive, Stephen Lewin 684 of 1877, scrapped 1935. New locomotive rebuilt by Alan Keef 2007; new boiler fitted 2011.
2. Replica of original Great Laxey Mine locomotive, Stephen Lewin 685 of 1877, scrapped 1935. New locomotive rebuilt by GLMR volunteers Winter 2008–09. Fitted with new boiler 2011. Both carry replica builder's plates from the 1877-built locomotives.

GREEN

Thomas Green & Son Ltd, Smithfield Foundry, North Street, Leeds.

Builder's No.	Year	Type	Class	Gauge	Location	Running No./ Name	Notes
441	1908	0-6-2ST		2ft	South Tynedale Railway	Barber	1

1. North Eastern Gas Board, Harrogate until 4/1957.

HORLOCK

A. Horlock & Co., North Fleet Iron Works, Undershore, Northfleet, Kent.

Builder's No.	Year	Type	Class	Gauge	Location	Running No./ Name	Notes
-	1848	0-4-0		4ft	National Trust, Penrhyn Castle	Fire Queen	1

1. Used on Padarn Railway until 1886 and preserved at Dinorwic Slate Quarries, Llanberis until1969. The only Crampton patent locomotive in the UK at present.

HUDSWELL, CLARKE

Hudswell, Clarke & Co. Lt, Railway Foundry, Hunslet, Leeds.

Builder's No.	Year	Type	Class	Gauge	Location	Running No./ Name	Notes
573	1900	0-4-0ST		3ft	National Railway Museum, York	Handyman	1
633	1902	0-4-0ST		3ft	Eastwell History Group	Lord Granby	2
639	1902	0-4-2ST		550mm	P. Rampton, Surrey	4 San Justo	3
640	1902	0-4-2ST		550mm	P. Rampton, Surrey	5 Santa Ana	3
972	1912	0-6-0		2ft	Statfold Barn Railway	No. 11 Fiji	4
1056	1914	0-4-0ST		2ft	Stafold Barn Railway	No. 19 Kanaka	5
1172	1915–24	0-6-0PT		2ft	P. Mason, Hampshire	Alpha	6
1238	1916	0-6-0WT	Ganges	2ft	Apedale Valley Light Railway	9	7
1643	1930	0-6-0WT		2ft	Statfold Barn Railway	GP 39	8

1. Staveley Minerals Ltd, Scaldwell Quarries, Northamptonshire until 5/1964.
2. Staveley Minerals Ltd, Eastwell Quarries, Leicestershire until 4/1961.
3. Repatriated from Spain 6/1973.
4. Repatriated from Fiji 2011, fitted with a diesel engine installed in the firebox area for use at a tourist railway. Rebuilt back to steam at Statfold Barn 2013-14.
5. Repatriated from Fiji 2012.
6. Repatriated from India 3/2013. Ordered for Rhodesia 5/1915, but cancelled. Remained unfinished until an order received from India. Then completed and despatched 5/1924.
7. Repatriated from Ghana 5/2008. Under restoration in a Yorkshire workshops; completion target 9/2014.
8. Penrhyn Quarries, Bethesda (Bronllwyd) until 1/1966 (where regauged to 1ft 10¾in). To Bressingham without a boiler; rebuilt there with boiler from Kerr Stuart 2395, since replaced by a new boiler.

HUGHES

Hughes Locomotive & Tramway Engine Works Ltd, Loughborough, Leicestershire.

Builder's No.	Year	Type	Class	Gauge	Location	Running No./ Name	Notes
323	1878	0-4-2ST		2ft 3in	The Engine House, Highley	No. 3 Sir Haydn	1

1. On loan from the Talyllyn Railway. Originally 0-4-0ST, rebuilt by Brush Electrical Engineering in 1900. Corris Railway, GWR and BR(W) No.3. To TR 3/1951. Sometimes carries the name Sir Handel.

▲▼ Great Northern Steam 21 of 2004, 1ft 7in gauge 0-4-0WT "Bee" is a new-build replica of one of the two original Laxey lead mines tramway locomotives, built for the 21st century Great Laxey Mines Railway. "Ant" and "Bee" each carry two builder's plates. **Peter Nicholson (2)**

▲ Hudswell Clarke 633 of 1902, 3ft gauge 0-4-0ST "Lord Granby" was an almost forgotten locomotive. In open-air storage at Leeds Industrial Museum it disappeared in undergrowth until enthusiasts cleared the site, revealing the loco, as seen on 9 April 2012. It is now at Eastwell, Leicestershire for static restoration. **Peter Nicholson**

▼ Hudswell Clarke 1172 of 1924, 0-6-0PT, is perhaps one of the least well-known narrow gauge steam locomotives in the UK. Imported from India in March 2013 and now at a private site in Hampshire, it is seen in as-arrived condition on 17 May 2013. **Phil Mason**

HUNSLET

Hunslet Engine Co Ltd, Leeds.

Builder's No.	Year	Type	Class	Gauge	Location	Running No./ Name	Notes
283	1882	0-4-0ST		1ft 11½in	National Trust, Penrhyn Castle	*Charles*	1
316	1883	0-4-0ST+T	Port	2ft	Bressingham	*Gwynedd*	2
317	1883	0-4-0ST+T	Port	600mm	Launceston Steam Railway	*Lilian*	3
364	1885	0-4-0ST	Port	1ft 11½in	Bala Lake Railway	*Winifred*	4
409	1886	0-4-0ST	Alice	600mm	Launceston Steam Railway	*Velinheli*	5
492	1888	0-4-0ST	Alice	1ft 10¾in	Ffestiniog Railway	*King of the Scarlets*	6
493	1889	0-4-0ST	Alice	1ft 11½in	Llanberis Lake Railway	No. 1 *Elidir*	7
541	1891	0-4-0ST	Alice	1ft 10¾in	Narrow Gauge Railway Museum	*Rough Pup*	8
542	1891	0-4-0ST	Alice	2ft	Purbeck Mineral & Mining Museum	*Cloister*	9
554	1891	0-4-0ST	Lilla	1ft 11½in	Ffestiniog Railway	*Lilla*	10
555	1892	2-6-2T		3ft	Tralee & Dingle Steam Railway	No. 5T	11
589	1893	2-4-0ST+T	Mainline	1ft 11½in	Ffestiniog Railway	*Blanche*	12
590	1893	2-4-0ST+T	Mainline	1ft 11½in	Ffestiniog Railway	*Linda*	13
605	1894	0-4-0ST	Small	2ft	Vale of Rheidol Railway	*Margaret*	14
606	1894	0-4-0ST	Small	2ft	Teifi Valley Railway	*Alan George*	15
638	1895	0-4-0ST	Mills	2ft	Hollycombe Steam Museum	*Jerry M.*	16
671	1898	0-4-0ST	Mills	1ft 10¾in	Thursford Collection	*Cackler*	17
678	1898	0-4-0ST	Port	2ft	Helical Technology Ltd, Lytham St Annes	*Jonathan*	18
679	1898	0-4-0ST+T	Port	600mm	Launceston Steam Railway	*Covertcoat*	19
680	1898	0-4-0ST	Alice	2ft	Bala Lake Railway	1 *George B*	20
684	1898	0-4-0WT		1ft 6in	Leeds Industrial Museum	*Jack*	21
705	1899	0-4-0ST	Small	1ft 11½in	J. Martin, Kent	*Elin*	22
707	1899	0-4-0ST		1ft 11½in	Ffestiniog Railway	1 *Britomart*	23
763	1901	0-4-0ST		600mm	Launceston Steam Railway	*Dorothea*	24
779	1902	0-4-0ST	Alice	1ft 11½in	Bala Lake Railway	No. 3 *Holy War*	25
780	1902	0-4-0ST	Alice	1ft 11½in	Bala Lake Railway	*Alice*	26
822	1903	0-4-0ST	Alice	1ft 11½in	Bala Lake Railway	*Maid Marian*	27
823	1903	0-4-0ST	Alice	2ft	West Lancashire Light Railway	*Irish Mail*	28
827	1903	0-4-0ST	Alice	1ft 11½in	Brecon Mountain Railway	*Sybil*	29
849	1904	0-4-0ST	Alice	1ft 11½in	Llanberis Lake Railway	No. 2 *Wild Aster/ Thomas Bach*	7
855	1904	0-4-0ST	Large	1ft 11½in	National Trust, Penrhyn Castle	*Hugh Napier*	30
873	1905	0-4-0ST		1ft 11½in	Welsh Slate Museum, Llanberis	*Una*	23
901	1906	2-6-2T		1ft 11½in	Welsh Highland Heritage Railway	*Russell*	31
920	1906	0-4-0ST	Large	2ft	Old Kiln Light Railway	*Pamela*	32
921	1906	0-4-0ST	Large	2ft	Statfold Barn Railway	*Sybil Mary*	33
994	1909	0-4-0ST	Large	2ft	Bressingham	*George Sholto*	34
996	1909	0-4-0ST	Large	2ft	A. Neal c/o Beamish	*Edward Sholto*	35
1215	1916	4-6-0T	War Office	2ft	Apedale Valley Light Railway	303	36
1429	1922	0-4-0ST	Port	2ft	Bredgar & Wormshill Lt Ry	*Lady Joan*	37
1430	1922	0-4-0ST	Port	1ft 11½in	Llanberis Lake Railway	No. 3 *Dolbadarn*	7
1709	1932	0-4-0ST	Late Port	1ft 10¾in	Statfold Barn Railway	*Michael*	6
1842	1936	0-4-2ST	Brazil	2ft	Statfold Barn Railway	*Josephine*	38
1859	1937	0-4-2T		2ft	Alan Keef Ltd	No. 16 *Carlisle*	39
2075	1940	0-4-2T		2ft	Toddington NG Railway	*Chaka's Kraal No. 6*	40
3815	1954	2-6-2T		2ft 6in	Locomotion, Shildon	No. 14 *SLR 85*	41
3902	1971	0-4-2ST	Brazil	2ft	Statfold Barn Railway	No. 4 *Trangkil No. 4*	42

1. Penrhyn Slate Quarries, Bethesda until 5/1963. Regauged from 1ft 10¾in.
2. Penrhyn Slate Quarries, Bethesda until 1964. Regauged from 1ft 10¾in. Under restoration for use at Bressingham and Penrhyn Quarry Railway.
3. Penrhyn Slate Quarries, Bethesda until 1965. Regauged from 1ft 10¾in. Fitted with tender 7/2008.

4. Penrhyn Slate Quarries, Bethesda until 1965. Repatriated from USA 4/2012. Regauged from 1ft 10¾in.
5. Dinorwic Slate Quarries, Llanberis until 1/1969. Regauged from 1ft 10¾in.
6. Dinorwic Slate Quarries, Llanberis until 1/1969. Repatriated from Canada 8/2012.
7. Dinorwic Slate Quarries, Llanberis until 12/1969. Regauged from 1ft 10¾in.
8. Dinorwic Slate Quarries, Llanberis until 6/1968.
9. Dinorwic Slate Quarries, Llanberis until 8/1962. Regauged from 1ft 10¾in.
10. Penrhyn Slate Quarries, Bethesda until 12/1963, where regauged to 1ft 10¾in 9/1934 – six years after arrival at Penrhyn second-hand! Regauged from 1ft 10¾in in 1971.
11. Originally Tralee & Dingle Railway, later Cavan & Leitrim Railway; Great Southern Railways Class PN2. Repatriated from USA in 1987.
12. Penrhyn Slate Quarries, Bethesda until 12/1963. Regauged from 1ft 10¾in. Fitted with tender 1964; rebuilt from 0-4-0ST 1972.
13. Penrhyn Slate Quarries, Bethesda until 7/1962. Regauged from 1ft 10¾in. Fitted with tender 1963; rebuilt from 0-4-0ST 1969.
14. Penrhyn Slate Quarries, Bethesda until 5/1968. Regauged from 1ft 10¾in.
15. Penrhyn Slate Quarries, Bethesda until 8/1965. Regauged from 1ft 10¾in.
16. Dinorwic Slate Quarries, Llanberis until 4/1967. Regauged from 1ft 10¾in.
17. Dinorwic Slate Quarries, Llanberis until 3/1966.
18. Dinorwic Slate Quarries, Llanberis until 7/1967. Regauged from 1ft 10¾in.
19. Dinorwic Slate Quarries, Llanberis until 12/1964. Regauged from 1ft 10¾in. Tender fitted 1991.
20. Dinorwic Slate Quarries, Llanberis until 10/1965. Regauged from 1ft 10¾in.
21. John Knowles (Wooden Box) Ltd, Woodville, Leicestershire until 10/1958.
22. Penrhyn Slate Quarries, Bethesda until 7/1962. Regauged from 1ft 10¾in.
23. Pen-yr-Orsedd Slate Quarry, Nantlle until 6/1965.
24. Dorothea Slate Quarry, Nantlle until 3/1970.
25. Dinorwic Slate Quarries, Llanberis until 3/1970. Regauged from 1ft 10¾in.
26. Dinorwic Slate Quarries, Llanberis until 11/1972. Regauged from 1ft 10¾in.
27. Dinorwic Slate Quarries, Llanberis until 5/1968. Regauged from 1ft 10¾in.
28. Dinorwic Slate Quarries, Llanberis until 11/1969. Acquired as main frame only and since rebuilt. Originally 1ft 10¾in gauge.
29. Pen-yr-Orsedd Slate Quarry, Nantlle until 9/1963.
30. Penrhyn SlateQuarries, Bethesda until 11/1966. Regauged from 1ft 10¾in.
31. New to North Wales Narrow Gauge Railways (later Welsh Highland Railway). Pike Bros, Fayle & Co. Ltd, Norden Clay Mines, Dorset until 8/1955.
32. Penrhyn Slate Quarries, Bethesda until 10/1966. Regauged from 1ft 10¾in.
33. Penrhyn Slate Quarries, Bethesda until 4/1966. Regauged from 1ft 10¾in.
34. Penrhyn Slate Quarries, Bethesda until 2/1966. Regauged from 1ft 10¾in.
35. Penrhyn Slate Quarries, Bethesda until 10/1961. The last new steam loco bought for Penrhyn Quarries. Repatriated from USA 7/2006. Regauged from 1ft 10¾in. Current base is Beamish, but visits other railways.
36. Originally WDLR No. 303. Repatriated from Australia 9/2005. Under restoration in a Yorkshire workshops; completion target 9/2014.
37. Dinorwic Slate Quarries, Llanberis until 2/1968. Regauged from 1ft 10¾in.
38. British Aluminium Co. Ltd, Lochaber Works, Fort William until 11/1969. Originally a 3ft gauge 0-4-2ST, but rebuilt as 0-4-2T and regauged by B. J. Curl, Hampshire. Rebuilt as a saddle tank again, at Statfold Barn 2014.
39. Repatriated from South Africa 1997. Under restoration for South Tynedale Railway, due for completion 2015. To be modified to burn wood waste briquettes.
40. Repatriated from South Africa 1981.
41. Repatriated from Sierra Leone 8/75 (Sierra Leone Government Railway No. 85); on loan from Welshpool & Llanfair Light Railway.
42. Repatriated from Java, Indonesia 2004. Regauged from 750mm. The last industrial steam locomotive built in UK.

HUNSLET (STATFOLD)

Hunslet Steam Co. Statfold Barn Farm, Ashby Road, Tamworth, Staffordshire.

Builder's No.	Year	Type	Class	Gauge	Location	Running No./ Name	Notes
3903	2005	0-4-0ST	Quarry	2ft	Statfold Barn Railway	*Statfold*	1
3904	2006	0-4-0ST	Quarry	2ft	Statfold Barn Railway	*Jack Lane*	1
3905	2007	0-4-0ST	Wren	2ft	Amerton Railway	*Jennie*	2
3906	2009	0-4-0ST	Wren	2ft	London Museum of Water & Steam	*Thomas Wicksteed*	3

1. The first two of a proposed batch of four new-build Hunslet Quarry tanks.
2. Completed at Statfold Barn in 2007, but builder's plate is dated 2005. Incorporates parts produced previously by the late Peter Lowe of the Abbey Light Railway, Leeds.
3. Construction started at Kew Bridge Steam Museum in 1995 and completed at Statfold Barn in 2009.

KEEF

Alan Keef Ltd, Lea Line, near Ross-on-Wye, Herefordshire (See also Section 6. New-build Locomotives Under Construction.)

Builder's No.	Year	Type	Class	Gauge	Location	Running No./ Name	Notes
-	1979	4wVB	Tram	2ft	Telford Horsehay Steam Trust		1
30	1994	0-4-0VBT		2ft	Alan Keef Ltd	*Taffy*	2
93R	2013	4wVBTG		2ft	Groudle Glen Railway		3

1. Construction started by Kierstead for Telford Development Corporation.
2. Construction started 1988 and completed in 1994, but builder's plate dated 1990.
3. Rebuilt from 4wD Motor Rail 5877 of 1935.

▲ Hughes 323 of 1878, 2ft 3in gauge 0-4-2ST is probably one of Britain's best-known narrow gauge steam locomotives. Originally Corris Railway No. 3, it is today Talyllyn Railway No. 3 "Sir Haydn". 'Out of ticket', it went on a publicity tour in 2013, as exhibited at Minehead station, West Somerset Railway on 5 October. **Peter Nicholson**

▲ Hunslet 317 of 1883, 0-4-0ST+T "Lilian" is one of many surviving North Wales Quarry Tanks built by Hunslet. Now 131 years old, it is a regular performer on the Launceston Steam Railway where seen on 15 July 2013 with owner Nigel Bowman at the controls. **Peter Nicholson**

▼ Hunslet 3902 of 1971, 0-4-2ST "Trangkil No. 4" is a historic locomotive because of its comparatively young age. Not only the last steam loco to be built at Hunslet's Jack Lane Works, Leeds, but the last of any gauge to be built in the UK for commercial industrial operation. Supplied to Indonesia it is now based at the Statfold Barn Railway, where it is seen on 1 June 2013. **Peter Nicholson**

KERR STUART

Kerr, Stuart & Co. Ltd, California Works, Stoke-on-Trent, Staffordshire.

Builder's No.	Year	Type	Class	Gauge	Location	Running No./ Name	Notes
720	1901	0-4-2		1ft 3in	Ravenglass & Eskdale Railway	11 *Bonnie Dundee*	1
721	1901	0-4-0WT		2ft	Narrow Gauge Railway Museum	No. 2	2
857/858?	1904	0-4-2ST	Maurice	2ft 6in	Corris Railway	(*Sir Neville Lubbock*)	3
886	1905	0-4-2ST	Brazil	2ft 6in	Sittingbourne & Kemsley Lt Ry	*Premier*	4
926	1905	0-4-2ST	Brazil	2ft 6in	Sittingbourne & Kemsley Lt Ry	*Leader*	4
1049	1908	0-4-2ST	Brazil	2ft 6in	Great Whipsnade Railway	No. 2 *Excelsior*	5
1098	1910	0-4-2ST	Brazil	2ft	FMB Engineering	No. 2 *Lena*	6
1158	1917	0-4-0T	Sirdar	2ft	P. Mason, Hampshire	*Diana*	7
1313	1916	0-4-2ST	Brazil	2ft	FMB Engineering	No. 6 *Lucy*	6
2395	1917	0-4-2ST	Tattoo	2ft	Apedale Valley Light Railway	*Stanhope*	8
2405	1915	0-6-0WTT	Joffre	2ft	West Lancashire Light Railway	No. 8 *Joffre*	9
2442	1915	0-6-0WTT	Joffre	600mm	J. Martin, Kent		9
2451	1915	0-6-0WTT	Joffre	2ft	Lynton & Barnstaple Railway	*Axe*	10
3010	1916	0-6-0WTT	Joffre	600mm	Statfold Barn Railway	3010	9
3014	1916	0-6-0WTT	Joffre	2ft	Apedale Valley Light Railway		9
3024	1916	0-4-2T	Brazil	3ft	Cavan & Leitrim Railway	1 *Dromad*	11
3025	1917	0-4-2ST	Brazil	2ft 6in	FMB Engineering, Hampshire	1 *Edith*	3
3114	1918	0-4-0ST	Wren	2ft	Vale of Rheidol Railway	3114	12
3117	1918	0-6-2T	Haig	1ft 11½in	Teifi Valley Railway	*Sgt Murphy*	13
4034	1920	0-6-2T	Baretto	2ft 6in	Great Whipsnade Railway	No. 4 *Superior*	4
4047	1921	0-4-2ST	Tattoo	2ft 3in	Talyllyn Railway	No. 4 *Edward Thomas*	14
4219	1924	0-4-2ST	Brazil	2ft 6in	Sittingbourne & Kemsley Lt Ry	*Melior*	4
4250	1922	0-4-0ST	Wren	2ft	Amerton Railway	*Lorna Doone*	15
4256	1922	0-4-0ST	Wren	2ft	Leighton Buzzard Railway	*Peter Pan*	16
4260	1922	0-4-0ST	Wren	2ft	Leighton Buzzard Railway	*Pixie*	17
4404	1927	0-6-2T	Matary	2ft 6in	Welshpool & Llanfair Lt Ry	12 *Joan*	18
4408	1928	0-6-4T	ML	2ft 6in	Vale of Rheidol Railway, Surrey	695	19

1. Scottish Gas Board, Dundee Works until 10/1959. Built as 0-4-0WT. Regauged from 2ft in 1976; rebuilt as 0-4-2T by Ravenglass & Eskdale Railway 1981. Rebuilt as 0-4-2 by RER in 1996.
2. Scottish Gas Board, Dundee Works until 10/1959.
3. Repatriated from Antigua 10/2013. Identity of 857 or 858 to be confirmed. To be regauged to 2ft 3in
4. Bowaters UK Pulp & Paper Mills Ltd, Sittingbourne until 10/1969.
5. Bowaters UK Pulp & Paper Mills Ltd, Sittingbourne until 1/1969.
6. Imported from Antigua 8/2014. Stored in containers, for sale.
7. Pen-yr-Orsedd Slate Quarry, Nantlle until 8/1964.
8. Penrhyn Slate Quarries, Bethesda 1966. Dismantled parts to Bressingham where boiler and fittings were used on Hudswell Clarke 1643. The main frame was dismantled but these parts acquired by Brian Gent (FMB Engineering Co.) in 1992, and with Dave Eaves of Prototype Developments and Alan Keef Ltd, missing parts were located or manufactured with the loco being completed to running order in 1999.
9. Repatriated from France 10/74.
10. Repatriated from France 10/74. Major components, excluding main frame and boiler, used in new-build locomotive by Gartell Light Railway on behalf of Lynton & Barnstaple Railway, completed in 2006 – as detailed under Gartell Light Railway. Fate of main frame not known.
11. British Aluminium Co. Ltd, Lochaber Works, Fort William until 11/1969. Originally 0-4-2ST; rebuilt as 0-4-2T by Alan Keef Ltd 1993 from dismantled remains.
12. Used on the Ashover Light Railway, Derbyshire. Stored by R.P. Beard, Brockamin, Worcestershire until 5/1959.
13. Penrhyn Slate Quarries until 7/1964. Originally 600mm, regauged to 1ft 10¾ in 1922 for use at Penrhyn. Rebuilt at Penrhyn 1932 to lower boiler and side tanks to improve stability. Regauged and rebuilt as 0-6-2T by Winson Engineering, Penrhyndeudraeth No. 9 of 1991.
14. Corris Railway, GWR and BR(W) No. 4. To TR 3/1951.
15. Devon County Council, Wilminstone Quarry, Tavistock until 12/1955.
16. Devon County Council, Beacon Down Quarry, Parracombe until 5/1959. Owned by G. Morris and frequently visits other railways in UK and on the Continent.
17. Devon County Council, Wilminstone Quarry, Tavistock until 7/1957.

18. Repatriated from Antigua 1971. Has a modified Matary/Baretto frame and running gear with a Huxley class boiler.
19. Repatriated from India 9/1995.

KITSON

Kitson & Co., Airedale Foundry, Leeds.

Builder's No.	Year	Type	Class	Gauge	Location	Running No./ Name	Notes
2551 T56	1882	0-4-0	Tram	3ft	Hull Streetlife Museum of Transport	1	1
T84	1883	0-4-0	Tram	3ft	Ulster Folk & Transport Museum	2	2

1. Originally Portstewart Tramway; taken over by Belfast & Northern Counties Railway 1/6/1897; Midland Railway from 1903, and Northern Counties Committee from 1/1/1923. Presented for preservation in 1939.
2. Originally Portstewart Tramway; taken over by Belfast & Northern Counties Railway 1/6/1897; Midland Railway from 1903, and Northern Counties Committee from 1/1/1923. Presented for preservation by Ulster Transport Authority 12/1953, going on display in 1955.

MANNING WARDLE

Manning, Wardle & Co. Ltd, Boyne Engine Works, Hunslet, Leeds.

Builder's No.	Year	Type	Class	Gauge	Location	Running No./ Name	Notes
1382	1897	0-4-0ST		1ft 10¾in	Narrow Gauge Railway Museum	Jubilee 1897	1
1675	1906	0-6-0ST		3ft	Welland Valley Vintage Traction Club, Market Harborough	Kettering Furnaces No. 8	2
1877	1915	0-6-2T		2ft 6in	Great Whipsnade Railway	No. 1 Chevallier	3

1. Penrhyn Slate Quarries, Bethesda until 12/1963.
2. Kettering Iron & Coal Co. Ltd until 8/1963. Completely dismantled for restoration.
3. Bowaters UK Pulp & Paper Mills Ltd, Sittingbourne until 10/1968.

NASMYTH, WILSON

Nasmyth, Wilson & Co. Ltd, Bridgewater Foundry, Patricroft, Manchester.

Builder's No.	Year	Type	Class	Gauge	Location	Running No./ Name	Notes
828	1907	2-6-4T		3ft	Foyle Valley Railway Museum	No. 4 Meenglass	1
829	1907	2-6-4T		3ft	RPSI, Whitehead Depot	No. 5 Drumboe	2
830	1907	2-6-4T		3ft	Foyle Valley Railway Museum	6 Columbkille	1
956	1912	2-6-4T	Class 5A	3ft	Ulster Folk & Transport Museum	2 Blanche	3

1. County Donegal Railway Joint Committee until 1960.
2. County Donegal Railway Joint Committee until 1960. Under restoration for County Donegal Railway Restoration Ltd.
3. County Donegal Railway Joint Committee until 1961. Originally Class 2A.

NORTH BRITISH

North British Locomotive Co. Ltd, Glasgow.

Builder's No.	Year	Type	Class	Gauge	Location	Running No./ Name	Notes
17111	1906	4-6-2		2ft 6in	Vale of Rheidol Railway, Surrey	666	1
25546	1945	4-8-2	Class 15F	3ft 6in	Riverside Museum, Glasgow	3007	2
27271	1953	4-8-4	Class 25NC	3ft 6in	Buckinghamshire Railway Centre	3405 Janice	3
27770	1957	4-8-2+2-8-4	Class GMA	3ft 6in	Summerlee	4112	4

1. Repatriated from India 3/1995.
2. Built at Queen's Park Works. Repatriated from South Africa in 2006.

▲ Keef 30, 0-4-0VBT "Taffy" is a de Winton-type locomotive built between 1988 and 1994. Most components are new but it incorporates an original pair of cylinders and some motion parts. The works plate is dated 1990, about mid-way through the build. It is seen at Alan Keef's annual open day on 24 September 2011. **Peter Nicholson**

▼ Kerr Stuart 4047 of 1921 is a 'Tattoo' class 0-4-2ST built for the 2ft 3in gauge Corris Railway. Acquired by the Talyllyn Railway in 1951, No. 4 "Edward Thomas" is shown at Tywyn Wharf station on 5 May 2013. **Cliff Thomas**

▲ Kerr Stuart 4256 of 1922, 'Wren' class 0-4-0ST "Peter Pan" has visited more railways than any other loco. Owned by Graham Morris it has been to most UK 2ft gauge heritage railways, worked on portable lines at many sites, and toured the Continent. It regularly attends the Devon Railway Centre's annual steam gala and is pictured here with resident Orenstein & Koppel 5744 of 1912, 0-4-0WT "Rebecca" on 18 August 2013.   **Peter Nicholson**

▼ Manning Wardle 1877 of 1915. 0-6-2T "Chevallier" was built for the 2ft 6in gauge military Chattenden & Upnor Railway, Kent, then bought by Bowaters of Sittingbourne. Now privately owned it is seen on the Great Whipsnade Railway on 27 July 2011.   **Cliff Thomas**

3. Built at Hyde Park Works. Repatriated from South Africa 10/1991.
4. Built at Hyde Park Works. Order subcontracted from Beyer Peacock and given builder's No. 7827. Previously named *Springbok.* Repatriated from South Africa 7/1984.

NORTH DORSET

North Dorset Locomotive Works, Motcombe, near Shaftesbury, Dorset.

Builder's No.	Year	Type	Class	Gauge	Location	Running No./ Name	Notes
698	1998	0-4-2T		2ft	Gartell Light Railway	No. 6 *Mr. G*	1

1. Built over a six-year period by John Uphill and Dr Alan White.

PECKETT

Peckett & Sons Ltd, Atlas Locomotive Works, St George, Bristol.

Builder's No.	Year	Type	Class	Gauge	Location	Running No./ Name	Notes
783	1899	0-4-0ST	M4	4ft 6in	Wheal Martyn	*Lee Moor No. 1*	1
784	1899	0-4-0ST	M4	4ft 6in	South Devon Railway	*Lee Moor No. 2*	1
1008	1903	0-6-0ST	Jurassic	2ft	Lincolnshire Coast Light Railway	2 *Jurassic*	2
1026	1904	0-4-0T	Aluminium	3ft	Giants Causeway & Bushmills Ry	No. 1 *Tyrone*	3
1097	1906	0-4-0T	Aluminium	3ft	Ulster Folk & Transport Museum	2	4
1270	1911	0-6-0ST	Jurassic	1ft 11½in	Statfold Barn Railway	*Triassic*	5
1316	1913	0-6-0ST	11in	3ft	Amberley Museum	*Scald*well	6
1327	1913	0-6-0ST	Jurassic	2ft	R. Palmer, Bromyard, Herefordshire *Mesozoic*		7
1632	1923	0-6-0ST	Jurassic	2ft	Statfold Barn Railway	*Liassic*	8
1870	1934	0-6-0ST	M7	1000mm	Irchester NG Railway Mueseun	No. 85 1	9
1871	1934	0-6-0ST	M7	1000mm	Irchester NG Railway Museum	(No. 86)	10
2024	1942	0-4-2T		1ft 11½in	Welsh Highland Heritage Railway	*Karen*	11
2029	1942	0-6-0ST	SPL.R4	1000mm	Irchester NG Railway Museum	(No. 87) 8315/87	12
2050	1944	0-6-0ST	SPL.9½in	2ft	Statfold Barn Railway	No. 1 *Harrogate*	13

1. English Clays, Lovering Pochin & Co. Ltd, Lee Moor, Devon until 5/1964; withdrawn from use 11/1945.
2. Rugby Portland Cement Co. Ltd, Southam, Warwickshire until 6/1961.
3. British Aluminium Co. Ltd, Larne until 10/1960.
4. British Aluminium Co. Ltd Larne until 1955.
5. Rugby Portland Cement Co. Ltd, Southam, Warwickshire until 8/1957.
6. Staveley Minerals Ltd, Scaldwell Ironstone Quarries, Northamptonshire until 3/1964.
7. Rugby Portland Cement Co. Ltd, Southam, Warwickshire until 7/1961.
8. Rugby Portland Cement Co. Ltd, Southam, Warwickshire until 6/1959. Repatriated from Canada 8/2012.
9. Stewarts & Lloyds Minerals Ltd, Wellingborough Quarries, Northamptonshire until 12/1966.
10. Stewarts & Lloyds Minerals Ltd, Wellingborough Quarries, Northamptonshire until 6/1967.
11. Repatriated from Republic of Rhodesia 1972.
12. Stewarts & Lloyds Minerals Ltd, Wellingborough Quarries, Northamptonshire until 8/1967.
13. North Eastern Gas Board, Harrogate Works until 8/1957.

ROANOKE

Roanoke, Unit 2A, Grange Hill Industrial Estate, Bratton Fleming, Barnstaple, Devon EX31 4UH.

Builder's No.	Year	Type	Class	Gauge	Location	Running No./ Name	Notes
0507 ST	2004	0-4-0TVBG		2ft	John Spenceley, Cornwall		

ROBERT STEPHENSON

Robert Stephenson & Co. Ltd, Forth Street, Newcastle upon Tyne.

Builder's No.	Year	Type	Class	Gauge	Location	Running No./ Name	Notes
2613	1887	4-4-0T	Class DN2	3ft	Ulster Folk & Transport Museum	(2 *Kathleen*)	1

1. Cavan & Leitrim Railway; taken over by Great Southern Railways 1/1/1925; withdrawn as CIE No. 2L 1960; to preservation 12/1961.

ROBERT STEPHENSON & HAWTHORNS

Robert Stephenson & Hawthorns Ltd, Darlington Works, Co. Durham.

Builder's No.	Year	Type	Class	Gauge	Location	Running No./ Name	Notes
7430	1951	4-6-2		3ft 6in	Tanfield Railway	M2	1

1. Repatriated from Tasmania 7/92. Originally Tasmanian Government Railways No. M10.

SENTINEL

Sentinel Waggon Works (1920) Ltd, Harlescott, Shrewsbury, Shropshire.

Builder's No.	Year	Type	Class	Gauge	Location	Running No./ Name	Notes
7701	1929	4wTVBG		2ft 6in	Leighton Buzzard Railway	5 *Nutty* LBC L1	1

1. London Brick Co. Ltd, Hicks Works, Fletton, Peterborough until 6/1964. Regauged from 2ft 11in.

▲ North British 27291 of 1953, 3ft 6in gauge 4-8-4 No. 3405 "Janice" Is one of more than 100 Class 25NC locomotives built for South African Railways. The weight of loco and tender exceeds 200 tons. It is pictured at the Buckinghamshire Railway Centre on 17 February 2013. **Cliff Thomas**

SHARP, STEWART

Sharp, Stewart & Co. Ltd, Atlas Works, Glasgow.

Builder's No.	Year	Type	Class	Gauge	Location	Running No./ Name	Notes
3518	1888	0-4-0STWT+T		2ft	A. Shooter, Oxfordshire	19	1
4150	1896	4-8-0		3ft 6in	Locomotion, Shildon	993	2

1. Repatriated from the USA in 1/2003. Originally Darjeeling Himalayan Railway, until 1962.
2. Repatriated from Zambia 3/1975.

SPENCE

Wm Spence, Cork Street Foundry, Dublin.

Builder's No.	Year	Type	Class	Gauge	Location	Running No./ Name	Notes
13L	1895	0-4-0T		1ft 10in	Narrow Gauge Railway Museum	13	1
-	1902	0-4-0T		1ft 10in	Guinness Storehouse	17	2
-	1905	0-4-0T		1ft 10in	Ulster Folk & Transport Museum	20	3
-	1905	0-4-0T		1ft 10in	Garry Skelton, Galway	21	4
-	1912	0-4-0T		1ft 10in	Stradbally Steam Museum	15	5
-	1912	0-4-0T		1ft 10in	Irish NG Trust, Dromod	22	6
23L	1920	0-4-0T		1ft 10in	Amberley Museum	23	7

1. Arthur Guinness, Son & Co. (Dublin) Ltd, St James's Gate Brewery, Dublin until 8/1956.
2. Withdrawn from brewery tramway and placed in Guinness museum in 1962.
3. Arthur Guinness, Son & Co. (Dublin) Ltd, St James's Gate Brewery, Dublin until 1956.
4. Arthur Guinness, Son & Co. (Dublin) Ltd, St James's Gate Brewery, Dublin until c/1975.
5. Arthur Guinness, Son & Co. (Dublin) Ltd, St James's Gate Brewery, Dublin until 7/1966. Carries incorrectly dated builder's plate 1895. Originally No. 22, but renumbered when given the boiler from original No. 15.
6. Arthur Guinness, Son & Co. (Dublin) Ltd, St James's Gate Brewery, Dublin until ? Withdrawn from use 1957. Believed to originally have been No. 15 until boiler transferred to present No. 15 (ex-No. 22), and then renumbered 22. Now boilerless.
7. Arthur Guinness, Son & Co. (Dublin) Ltd, St James's Gate Brewery, Dublin until 11/1966. Preserved with 5ft 3in gauge converter bogie No. 4 and hoist.

WINSON

Winson Engineering, Daventry, Northamptonshire (see also Section 6 New-build Locomotives).

Builder's No.	Year	Type	Class	Gauge	Location	Running No./ Name	Notes
17	2005	0-4-2ST	Tattoo	2ft 3in	Corris Railway	No. 7	1

1. Replica of Kerr Stuart 4047 of 1921, original Corris Railway No. 4, now on the Talyllyn Railway. Construction started by Winson in 1999 and completed by former members of staff at Geo-Tek, Daventry after the company went into receivership 6/2001, and closed.

PLATFORM 5 MAIL ORDER

MINIATURE RAILWAYS
OF GREAT BRITAIN & IRELAND

The complete guide to all commercial miniature railways of gauges from 21"
to 7¼" that are open to the public and club tracks that open regularly to the
public.

For every railway a brief description of the line/circuit is provided, together with
details of location, address, gauge, line length, and contact details including
web addresses. Also included is a detailed listing of the resident locomotive
fleet for all commercial railways and most club tracks including details of:

- **Locomotive Numbers and Names Carried.**
- **Type of Locomotive (steam, battery, diesel, petrol).**
- **Transmission Type.**
- **Wheel Arrangement.**
- **Builder.**
- **Date of Construction.**

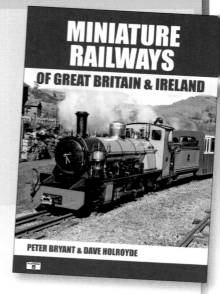

MINIATURE RAILWAYS OF GREAT BRITAIN & IRELAND

PETER BRYANT & DAVE HOLROYDE

Contains details of a remarkable 200 different
railway undertakings and well over 1000
different locomotives. 128 pages including over
60 colour illustrations. Published 2012. **£14.95**.

HOW TO ORDER
Telephone your order and credit/debit card details to our 24-hour sales orderline:
0114 255 8000 or Fax: 0114 255 2471. An answerphone is attached for calls made outside of normal UK office hours.
Or send your credit/debit card details, sterling cheque, money order or British Postal order payable to 'Platform 5 Publishing Ltd.' to:

**Mail Order Department (NGSL), Platform 5 Publishing Ltd,
52 Broadfield Road, SHEFFIELD, S8 0XJ, ENGLAND.**
Please add postage & packing: 10% UK; 20% Europe; 30% Rest of World. Please allow 28 days for delivery in the UK.

2. OVERSEAS LOCOMOTIVE BUILDERS

AUSTRALIA

FERNDALE

Ferndale Engineering (K. Watson and K. Tingle), Canning Vale, Western Australia.

Builder's No.	Year	Type	Class	Gauge	Location	Running No./ Name	Notes
21	2001	0-4-0ST		2ft	Leander Architectural, Derbyshire	*Phoenix*	1

1. Imported from Australia 8/2006. Carries fictitious builder's plate H. K. Porter, 18635 1896.

BELGIUM

COCKERILL

Société pour L'Exploitation des Establissements John Cockerill, Seraing.

Builder's No.	Year	Type	Class	Gauge	Location	Running No./ Name	Notes
3267	1937	2-6-2+2-6-2	NG/G16	2ft	Welsh Highland Railway	87	1

1. Imported from South Africa 1/1998.

▲ North Dorset Locomotive Works 698 of 1998, 0-4-2T No. 6 "Mr. G" was built for the Gartell Light Railway, the name referring to the late founder of the railway, Alan Gartell. It waits to leave Common Lane on 27 May 2013. **Peter Nicholson**

▲ Peckett 1316 of 1913, 3ft gauge 0-6-0ST "Scaldwell" is a former East Midlands ironstone quarry locomotive. Initially preserved at the now-closed Brockham Museum, Surrey, it is seen on static display at Amberley Museum on 10 July 2010. **Cliff Thomas**

▼ Pecketts 1632 of 1923 and 1270 of 1911, 'Jurassic' class 0-6-0STs "Liassic" and "Triassic" await restoration at the Statfold Barn Railway on 15 September 2012. Originating from Southam Cement Works, Warwickshire, four such locomotives are preserved. **Peter Nicholson**

COUILLET

Société Anonyme des Usines Metallurgiques du Haunaut, Couillet, Marcinelle, pres de Charleroi.

Builder's No.	Year	Type	Class	Gauge	Location	Running No./ Name	Notes
810	1885	0-4-0T		2ft	J. Martin, Kent	(Chuquintana)	1
1140	1895	0-6-0T		600mm	P. Rampton, Surrey	1 Sabero	2
1209	1898	0-6-0T		600mm	P. Rampton, Surrey	2 Samelices	2
1318	1900	0-6-0T		600mm	P. Rampton, Surrey	3 Olleros	2

1. Sold new as Decauville 36. Imported from Peru 2004. Regauged from 500mm.
2. Imported from Spain c1968.

FRANCO-BELGE (see also FRANCE)

Société Anglo-Franco-Belge des Ateliers de la Croyère, Seneffe & Godarville, Hainaut.

Builder's No.	Year	Type	Class	Gauge	Location	Running No./ Name	Notes
2667	1951	2-8-2	NG15	2ft	Welsh Highland Heritage Railway	120	1
2668	1951	2-8-2	NG15	2ft	Vale of Rheidol Railway, Surrey	121	2
2683	1952	2-8-2	NG15	2ft	Welsh Highland Railway	133	3
2684	1952	2-8-2	NG15	2ft	Welsh Highland Railway	134	3
2685	1952	2-8-2	NG15	2ft	Exmoor Steam Railway	135	4

1. Imported from South Africa 10/1994.
2. Imported from South Africa 7/1993.
3. Imported from South Africa 1/1998.
4. Imported from South Africa 12/1996.

LA MEUSE

Société Anonyme des Ateliers de Construction de la Meuse, Sclessin, Liége.

Builder's No.	Year	Type	Class	Gauge	Location	Running No./ Name	Notes
3243	1926	0-4-0T		2ft 6in	Statfold Barn Railway		1

1. Imported from Belgium 1990. Carries builder's plates 3355 of 1929.

CHINA

HARBIN

Harbin Forestry Machinery Factory, Harbin, Heilongjiang Province.

Builder's No.	Year	Type	Class	Gauge	Location	Running No./ Name	Notes
221	1988	0-8-0	Class C2	2ft 6in	Ffestiniog Railway	4	1

1. Imported from China1/2007. Completely dismantled.

FRANCE

CORPET LOUVET

Corpet, Louvet & Co., La Courneuve, Seine St Denis.

Builder's No.	Year	Type	Class	Gauge	Location	Running No./ Name	Notes
439	1884	0-6-0PT		600mm	Statfold Barn Railway	2 *Minas de Aller 2*	1
493	1888	0-6-0T		1000mm	Irchester NG Railway Museum	4 *Cambrai*	2

1. Completed in 1884 but builder's plate reads 1885. Imported from Spain 3/2011.
2. Eastwell & Waltham Ironstone Co. Ltd, Waltham Quarries, Eaton, Leicestershire until 12/1960.

DECAUVILLE

Société Nouvelle des Establissements Decauville Aine, Petit-Bourg, Corbeil, Essonne.

Builder's No.	Year	Type	Class	Gauge	Location	Running No./ Name	Notes
246	1897	0-4-2T		2ft	Bredgar & Wormshill Lt Railway	7 *Victory*	1
917	1915	0-4-0TWT	Progres'	2ft	Leadhills & Wanlockhead Railway		2
1027	1926	0-4-0T		2ft	Vale of Rheidol Railway, Capel Bangor		3
1126	1947	0-4-0WT		2ft	Amberley Museum	*Barbouilleur*	4
1735	1919	0-6-0T		2ft	Statfold Barn Railway		5

1. Imported from Australia 1996.
2. Imported from France 3/2001.
3. Imported from France 4/2001.
4. Imported from France 1981.
5. Imported from Mozambique 11/2000.

▲ Roanoke 0507 ST of 2004, 0-4-0TVBG is a unique locomotive insofar as Roanoke usually builds miniature railway locos, traction engines and steam lorries. This example was built to the special order of John Spenceley, seen at the controls, for use on his private farm railway in Cornwall. Photographed with permission for this book, on 14 June 2014. **Peter Nicholson**

FRANCO-BELGE (see also BELGIUM)

Société Franco-Belge de Matériel de Chemins de Fer, Raismes, Nord.

Builder's No.	Year	Type	Class	Gauge	Location	Running No./ Name	Notes
2855	1944	0-8-0T		2ft 6in	Welshpool & Llanfair Light Railway	10 699.01 Sir Drefaldwyn	1

1. Imported from Austria 12/1969.

GERMANY

ARN. JUNG

Arn. Jung Lokomotivfabrik GmbH, Jungenthal-an-der-Sieg, Kirchen.

Builder's No.	Year	Type	Class	Gauge	Location	Running No./ Name	Notes
939	1906	0-4-0WT		2ft	Toddington NG Railway	Justine	1
1261	1908	0-6-2WT+T		1ft 11¾in	Brecon Mountain Railway	Graf Schwerin-Lowitz	2
2279	1914	0-4-4-0T		750mm	Statfold Barn Railway	5 Tjepper	3
2569	1918	0-4-0WT		600mm	J. Martin, Kent	Anne-Marie	4
3175	1921	0-4-0WT		2ft	J. Martin, Kent	Jenny	5
3872	1931	0-6-0WT		2ft	Bredgar & Wormshill Lt Railway	2 Katie	6
4878	1930	0-4-4-0T		2ft	Statfold Barn Railway	9 Sf. Djatibarang	3
7509	1937	0-4-0WT		1ft 11½in	Strumpshaw Steam Museum	No. 6 Ginette Marie	7

1. Imported from Belgium 7/1975.
2. Imported from East Germany 1973.
3. Imported from Indonesia 1/2006.
4. Imported from France.
5. Imported from Argentina 7/03.
6. Imported from British Cameroons 1973.
7. Imported from Germany 12/1971.

BERLINER/SCHWARTZKOPFF

Berliner Maschinenbau AG, formerly L. Schwartzkopff, Berlin.

Builder's No.	Year	Type	Class	Gauge	Location	Running No./ Name	Notes
9124	1927	0-4-0WT		2ft	Bredgar & Wormshill Lt Railway	1 Bronhilde	1

1. Imported from Germany in 1976.

BORSIG

A. Borsig GmbH, Berlin.

Builder's No.	Year	Type	Class	Gauge	Location	Running No./ Name	Notes
5913	1908	0-4-0WT		600mm	Vale of Rheidol Railway, Surrey		1
6022	1906	0-6-2T		600mm	P. Rampton, Surrey	7 Sotillos	2

1. Imported from Belgium 1994.
2. Imported from Spain c1968.

FREUDENSTEIN

Stahlbahnwerke Freudenstein & Co., Templehof, Dortmund, Berlin.

Builder's No.	Year	Type	Class	Gauge	Location	Running No./ Name	Notes
73	1901	0-4-0WT		2ft	Leighton Buzzard Railway	*Penlee*	1

1. Original locomotive used at Penlee Quarries Ltd, Newlyn, Cornwall and preserved on site from 1951. Rebuilt with new main frame by ARC *c*1983.

HANOMAG

Hannoversche Maschinenbau AG (formerly George Egestorff), Linden vor Hannover.

Builder's No.	Year	Type	Class	Gauge	Location	Running No./ Name	Notes
8282	1917	0-8-0T		600mm	R. Gambrill, Hampshire		1
8310	1918	0-8-0T		2ft	Statfold Barn Railway		2
10629	1928	2-6-2+2-6-2	NG/G13	1ft 11½in	Exmoor Steam Railway	77	3
10634	1928	2-6-2+2-6-2	NG/G13	600mm	P. Rampton, Surrey	(NG82)	4

1. Originally DFB. Imported from Mozambique 10/1998.
2. Originally DFB. Imported from France 1975.
3. Imported from S. Africa 1986.
4. Imported from South Africa 8/1978.

HENSCHEL

Henschel & Sohn GmbH, Kassel.

Builder's No.	Year	Type	Class	Gauge	Location	Running No./ Name	Notes
5276	1899	0-4-0F	Tram	1000mm	Alan Keef Ltd	No. 4 *Rur*	1
14019	1916	0-8-0T		600mm	Amerton Railway	3 (DFB 526)	2
14676	1917	0-8-0T		600mm	West Lancashire Railway	47	2
14928	1917	0-8-0T		600mm	Statfold Barn Railway	3 (DFB 998)	2
14968	1917	0-8-0T		600mm	Toddington NG Railway	15	2
15540	1917	0-8-0T		600mm	Penrhyn Quarry Railway Project	1	2
15968	1918	0-8-0T		2ft	Toddington NG Railway	1091 (DFB 1091)	3
16043	1918	0-4-0T		600mm	P. Rampton, Surrey	102	4
16045	1918	0-4-0T		600mm	P, Rampton, Surrey	103	4
16047	1918	0-4-0WT+T	90hp	2ft	South Tynedale Railway	125 *Thomas Edmondson*	5
16073	1918	0-4-2T		600m	P. Rampton, Surrey	101	4
28035	1948	0-4-0WT	70hp Riesa	2ft	South Tynedale Railway	*Helen Kathryn*	6
29582	1956	0-6-0WT		750mm	Bredgar & Wormshill Lt Ry	No. 105 *Siam*	7
29587	1957	2-8-2	NG15	2ft	P. Rampton, Surrey	146	8

1. Under restoration for the Selfkantbahn near Aachen; arrived UK 9/2013. Converted to a fireless loco in 1942 and being restored to original, ex-works condition. Due to return to Germany 2014.
2. Originally DFB. Imported from Mozambique 10/1998.
3. Originally DFB. Imported from Poland in 1985.
4. Imported from Spain *c*1968.
5. Imported from Spain 4/1984.
6. Imported from East Germany in 1971.
7. Imported from Thailand *c*1982.
8. Imported from South Africa.

▲ Sentinel 7701 of 1929, "Nutty", 2ft 6in gauge 4wTVBG, is the only extant narrow gauge Sentinel locomotive in the UK. Owned by the Narrow Gauge Railway Museum Trust it is on loan to the Leighton Buzzard Railway for static display, and seen at Stonehenge Works on 15 September 2012.
Cliff Thomas

▼ Sharp Stewart 3518 of 1888, 0-4-0STWT+T is former Darjeeling Himalayan Railway No. 19, repatriated from India via the USA. It can sometimes be seen in action on Adrian Shooter's private Beeches Light Railway by pre-booked parties. Such an occasion was on 21 June 2014. **Dennis Graham**

▲ Winson 17 of 2005, is a new-build Kerr Stuart 'Tattoo' class 0-4-2ST built for the 2ft 3in gauge Corris Railway. Photographed at Corris station on 5 May 2013, it is a replacement for the original Corris No. 4 that is now at the Talyllyn Railway. **Cliff Thomas**

▼ Cockerill 3267 of 1937, 2-6-2+2-6-2 No. 87 is one of the ex-South African Railways NG/G16 class Beyer-Garratt locomotives imported from South Africa now operating on the demanding Welsh Highland Railway, between Caernarfon and Porthmadog. It is seen arriving at Waunfawr with a southbound service on a very wet 23 August 2009. **Peter Nicholson**

KRAUSS

Lokomotivfabrik Krauss & Co., Sendeling Works, Munich.

Builder's No.	Year	Type	Class	Gauge	Location	Running No./ Name	Notes
4045	1899	0-4-2T+T		2ft	Statfold Barn Railway	No. 1 *Sragi No. 1*	1
7455	1918	0-8-0T		600mm	Leighton Buzzard Railway		2

1. Imported from Indonesia 11/2004.
2. Originally DFB. No. 2023.To be imported from France late 2014.

MAFFEI

J. A. Maffei AG, Munich.

Builder's No.	Year	Type	Class	Gauge	Location	Running No./ Name	Notes
4766	1917	0-8-0T		2ft	Vale of Rheidol Railway, Capel Bangor		1

1. Originally DFB. Imported from France 4/2001.

ORENSTEIN & KOPPEL

Orenstein & Koppel AG, Berlin.

Builder's No.	Year	Type	Class	Gauge	Location	Running No./ Name	Notes
614	1900	0-4-0WT+T	30hp	750mm	Statfold Barn Railway	1	1
1473	1905	0-4-4-0T	60hp	750mm	Statfold Barn Railway	5	1
2343	1907	0-6-0T	150hp	2ft	Statfold Barn Railway	740 *Matheran*	2
2378	1907	0-4-0WT	30hp	2ft	West Lancashire Light Railway	*Utrillas*	3
2544	1907	0-4-0WT	50hp	600mm	Leighton Buzzard Railway		4
3136	1908	0-4-0WT	40hp	2ft	J. Martin, Kent	No. 2 *Susan*	5
5102	1912	0-4-0WT	140hp	900mm	Alan Keef Ltd, Ross-on-Wye		6
5662	1912	0-4-0WT+T	50hp	600mm	Brookside Engine Co. Whaley Bridge	5662	7
5668	1912	0-4-0WTT	30hp	2ft	Bredgar & Wormshill Lt Railway	6 *Eigiau*	8
5744	1912	0-4-0WT	20hp	2ft	Devon Railway Centre	No. 14 *Rebecca*	9
5834	1912	0-4-0WT	20hp	2ft	Leighton Buzzard Railway	No. 11 *P. C. Allen*	10
6335	1913	0-4-0WT	50hp	2ft	Leadhills & Wanlockhead Railway	9 *Charlotte*	11
6641	1913	0-4-0WT	30hp	2ft	West Lancashire Light Railway	*Montalban*	3
7122	1914	0-6-0WT+T	40hp	2ft	D. Hamer, Kent	8 *Elsa*	12
7529	1914	0-4-0WT	50hp	2ft	Golden Valley Light Railway	2	13
8356	1917	0-8-0T	60hp	600mm	R. Gambrill, Hampshire		14
9239	1921	0-6-0WT	40hp	2ft	Ffestiniog Railway	(*Fojo*)	15
9922	1922	0-4-0WT	50hp	600mm	Willenhall Commercials, West Midlands	4	16
9998	1922	0-6-0WT	50hp	2ft	Old Kiln Light Railway	M. N. No. 1 *Elouise*	17
10701	1924	0-4-0WT	50hp	600mm	Willenhall Commercials, West Midlands	5	16
10750	1923	0-6-0WT	30hp	2ft	Statfold Barn Railway	*Sragi 14 Max*	18
10808	1924	0-6-0WT	90hp	2ft	Leighton Buzzard Railway	*Pedemoura*	15
10956	1925	0-10-0T	90hp	600mm	Preston Services, Canterbury, Kent	T907	19
10957	1925	0-10-0T	90hp	600mm	Preston Services, Canterbury, Kent	T912	19
11009	1925	0-6-0WT	90hp	600mm	J. Forshaw, Bedfordshire	1 *Veracruz*	20
11309	1927	0-10-0T	90hp	2ft	Preston Services, Canterbury, Kent		21
11784	1928	0-6-0WT	40hp	2ft	Great Bush Railway	*Sao Domingos*	15
12470	1934	0-10-0T	90hp	600mm	Preston Services, Canterbury, Kent	T908	19
12722	1936	0-4-0WT	50hp	2ft	Bredgar & Wormshill Lt Rly	8 *Helga*	22
12740	1936	0-6-0WT	50hp	2ft	Leighton Buzzard Railway	*Elf*	23
13101	1938	0-10-0T	90hp	600mm	Preston Services, Canterbury, Kent	T911	19

1. Imported from Indonesia 9/2004
2. Imported from India 1986.
3. Imported from Spain c1984.
4. Imported from Belgium 7/2003.
5. Imported from Belgium 2008. Carries boiler No. 11527.
6. Imported from Belgium in 1990. Kept in store for owner.
7. Imported from Argentina 7/2003.
8. Penrhyn Slate Quarries, Bethesda until 2/1963. Regauged to 1ft 10¾ for use at Penrhyn and rebuilt there 1930, converting side bunkers into water tanks. Regauged back to 2ft.
9. Imported from Argentina c3/2005.
10. Imported from Spain 1963.
11. Imported from Belgium in 1994. Kept in a locked container and not readily viewable.
12. Imported from Zimbabwe 1989.
13. Imported from France 11/1967.
14. Originally DFB. Imported from Mozambique 10/1998.
15. Imported from Portugal 1972.
16. Imported from Peru 2012.
17. Imported from Portugal c1969.
18. Imported from Indonesia 11/2004.
19. Imported from Argentina 1/2006
20. Imported from Peru 2011.
21. imported from Argentina 2003.
22. Imported from Germany 1969.
23. Imported from Cameroon 1971.

▲ Franco-Belge 2683 of 1952, 2-8-2 No. 133 is a former South African Railways NG15 class, imported for the Welsh Highland Railway. It is pictured on display in front of Caernarfon Castle on 24 August 2009, minus its tender. **Peter Nicholson**

PLATFORM 5 MAIL ORDER
EUROPEAN HANDBOOKS

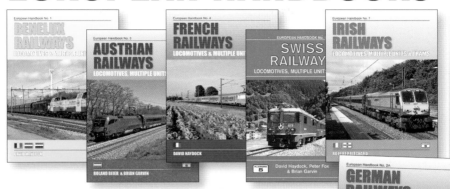

The Platform 5 European Railway Handbooks are the most comprehensive guides to the rolling stock of selected European railway administrations available. Each book lists all locomotives and railcars of the country concerned, giving details of number carried and depot allocation, together with a wealth of technical data for each class of vehicle. Each book is A5 size, thread sewn and includes at least 32 pages of colour illustrations. The Irish book also contain details of hauled coaching stock.

EUROPEAN HANDBOOKS CURRENTLY AVAILABLE:

No. 1 Benelux Railways (2012) £20.95
No. 2A German Railways Part 1: Deutsche Bahn (2013) £22.95
No. 2B German Railways Part 2: (NEW EDITION IN PREPARATION)
No. 3 Austrian Railways (2012) £19.95
No. 4 French Railways (2011) £19.95
No. 5 Swiss Railways (NEW EDITION IN PREPARATION)
No. 6 Italian Railways (NEW EDITION IN PREPARATION)
No. 7 Irish Railways (2013) £15.95
No. 8 Czech & Slovak Railways (IN PREPARATION)

HOW TO ORDER

Telephone your order and credit/debit card details to our 24-hour sales hotline:
0114 255 8000 (UK) + 44 114-255-8000 (from overseas) or Fax: +44(0)114-255-2471.
An answerphone is attached for calls made outside of normal UK office hours.
Please state type of card, card number, issue no./date (maestro cards only), expiry date and full name & address of cardholder.
Or send your credit/debit card details, sterling cheque or British Postal order payable to Platform 5 Publishing Ltd. to:

Mail Order Department (NGSL), Platform 5 Publishing Ltd., 52 Broadfield Road, SHEFFIELD, S8 0XJ, ENGLAND
Please add postage & packing: 10% UK; 20% Europe; 30% Rest of World.

▲ Harbin 221 of 1988, 2ft 6in gauge 0-8-0 was imported from China in 2007 and is seen in the Ffestiniog Railway's Boston Lodge Works on 2 May 2010, prior to complete dismantling, in which state it remains today. **Cliff Thomas**

▼ Corpet Louvet 439 of 1884, 0-6-0PT is of unusual appearance as it is fitted with Brown's valve gear using indirect drive via a rocker arm. It has been restored to as-built condition at Statfold Barn Railway, as can be seen in this view taken on 15 September 2012. **Peter Nicholson**

POLAND

FABLOK (CHRZANOW)

Fabryka Lokomotyw Imf Dzierzynskiego, Chrzanów.

Builder's No.	Year	Type	Class	Gauge	Location	Running No./ Name	Notes
2959	1951	0-6-0WT		750mm	Private, Buckinghamshire		1
3297	1954	0-6-0T	LAS	600mm	North Norfolk Railway		2
3326	1954	0-6-0WT		750mm	Private, Mid-Wales		1
3459	1957	0-6-0WT+T 70hp	LAS	2ft	South Tynedale Railway	10 *Naklo*	3
3506	1957	0-6-0T		2ft	West Lancashire Light Railway		4
3512	1957	0-6-0T		2ft	R. Gambrill, Hampshire	*Tourska*	5

1. Imported from Poland 6/1992; initially based at the Midland Railway-Butterley; 2959 then thought to be 1983 of 1949.
2. Imported 2014 for restoration on behalf of Stoomcentrum Maldegem, Belgium. Also at NNR for restoration is an unidentified 0-4-0, No. 9 *Aquila*.
3. Imported from Poland 4/1998. Originally 0-6-0WTT, tender added later; rebuilt in 2001without side tanks.
4. Imported from Poland 4/1998
5. Imported from Belgium. Carries plate: Fabrika Kotlow Toron 1966 of 1957.

ROMANIA

RESITA

Uzinele de Fier si Domenlile den Resita Societate Anonima, Resita.

Builder's No.	Year	Type	Class	Gauge	Location	Running No./ Name	Notes
1679	1954	0-8-0T		2ft 6in	Welshpool & Llanfair Light Railway	(764.423)	1
1681	1954	0-8-0T		2ft 6in	Welshpool & Llanfair Light Railway	(764.425)	2

1. Imported from Romania 2008. Builder's details subject to doubt.
2. Imported from Romania 2007. Builder's details subject to doubt.

SPAIN

SABERO

Hulleras de Sabero Y Anexas S.A., Sabero.

Builder's No.	Year	Type	Class	Gauge	Location	Running No./ Name	Notes
-	c1937	0-6-0T		600mm	Vale of Rheidol Railway, Surrey	6 *La Herrera*	1

1. Assembled from parts supplied by Couillet, France. Imported from Spain c1968.

SWITZERLAND

SLM

Schweizerische Lokomotive-und Maschinenfabrick, Winterthur.

Builder's No.	Year	Type	Class	Gauge	Location	Running No./ Name	Notes
924	1895	0-4-2T	Rack	800mm	Snowdon Mountain Railway	2 *Enid*	1
925	1895	0-4-2T	Rack	800mm	Snowdon Mountain Railway	3 *Wyddfa*	1
988	1896	0-4-2T	Rack	800mm	Snowdon Mountain Railway	4 *Snowdon*	1
989	1896	0-4-2T	Rack	800mm	Snowdon Mountain Railway	5 *Moel Siabod*	1
2838	1922	0-4-2T	Rack	800mm	Snowdon Mountain Railway	6 *Padarn*	1
2869	1923	0-4-2T	Rack	800mm	Snowdon Mountain Railway	7 *Ralph*	1
2870	1923	0-4-2T	Rack	800mm	Snowdon Mountain Railway	8 *Eryri*	1
-	1944	0-4-0WT		2ft	Private, Northamptonshire		2

1. Delivered new to the SMR.
2. Either SLM 3854 or 3855. Imported from Mozambique 8/1999.

▲ Decauville 246 of 1897, 0-4-2T was one of a pair supplied to Queensland, Australia for use in the sugar industry. Following import by the Bredgar & Wormshill Light Railway it was restored and is seen running on to the turntable there on 20 April 2014. **Peter Nicholson**

UNITED STATES OF AMERICA

ALCO

American Locomotive Co., Cooke Works, Paterson, New Jersey.

Builder's No.	Year	Type	Class	Gauge	Location	Running No./ Name	Notes
57156	1916	2-6-2T		1ft 11½in	Ffestiniog Railway	*Mountaineer*	1

1. Originally WDLR No. 1265. Imported from France 7/1965.

BALDWIN

Baldwin Locomotive Works, Philadelphia, Pennsylvania.

Builder's No.	Year	Type	Class	Gauge	Location	Running No./ Name	Notes
15515	1897	2-6-2		1ft 11¾in	Brecon Mountain Railway	1 *Santa Teresa*	1
44656	1917	4-6-0PT	10-12-D	2ft	Leighton Buzzard Railway	778	2
44657	1916	4-6-0PT	10-12-D	2ft	Statfold Barn Railway		3
44699	1917	4-6-0PT	10-12-D	2ft	Alan Keef Ltd		4
45190	1917	4-6-0PT	10-12-D	2ft	West Lancashire Light Railway		5
61269	1930	4-6-2		1ft 11¾in	Brecon Mountain Railway	2	6

1. Imported from Brazil 1990. Originally a 2ft gauge 2-6-0, but ran for a while in Brazil as 2ft 6in gauge. Rebuilt as a 2-6-2 by BMR.
2. Originally WDLR No. 778. Imported from India 1985.
3. Originally WDLR No. 779. Imported from India 3/2013.
4. Originally WDLR No. 794. Imported from India 1985. Owned by the Imperial War Museum, but being restored for use on the Welsh Highland Heritage Railway as WHR No. 590.
5. Originally WDLR No. 1058. Imported from India 3/2013.
6. Imported from South Africa 7/1974 as an insurance write-off following an accident.

DAVENPORT

Davenport Locomotive Works, Davenport, Iowa.

Builder's No.	Year	Type	Class	Gauge	Location	Running No./ Name	Notes
1586	1917	0-4-0		2ft	Statfold Barn Railway		1

1. Imported from India 2013.

3. LOCOMOTIVES BUILT BY OWNERS AND OPERATORS

(See also Section 4 Homebuilt 'Coffee Pot' vertical boiler locomotives.)

R. BOOTH

Douglas, Isle of Man.

Builder's No.	Year	Type	Class	Gauge	Location	Running No./ Name	Notes
-	1998	0-4-2T		2ft	Groudle Glen Railway	*Annie*	1

1. Replica of Bagnall 1922 of 1911 built for the Gentle Annie Tramway, Gisbourne, New Zealand.

A. B. M. BRAITHWAITE AND BRESSINGHAM STEAM PRESERVATION CO.

Granta Technology Park, Cambridge and Bressingham, near Diss, Norfolk.

Builder's No.	Year	Type	Class	Gauge	Location	Running No./ Name	Notes
2	2009	0-4-0ST+T		2ft	Bressingham	No. 2 *Bevan*	1

1. Designed by Bevan Braithwaite and completed at Bressingham following his death in 4/2008.

▲ Arn. Jung 939 of 1906, 0-4-0WT normally operates on the Toddington Narrow Gauge Railway, Gloucestershire, but is seen here visiting to Alan Keef's open day on 26 September 2009. It is propelling Penrhyn slate quarrymen's coach 'H'.   **Peter Nicholson**

T. D. A. CIVIL

Near Uttoxeter, Staffordshire.

Builder's No.	Year	Type	Class	Gauge	Location	Running No./ Name	Notes
1	1997	0-4-2IST		2ft	Golden Valley Light Railway	*Joan*	1

1. Replica of a Bagnall inverted saddle tank. Originally named *Pearl 2*.

FESTINIOG RAILWAY

Boston Lodge Works, Portmadoc/Porthmadog.

Builder's No.	Year	Type	Class	Gauge	Location	Running No./ Name	Notes
-	1879	0-4-4-0T		1ft 11½in	Ffestiniog Railway	No. 10 *Merddin Emrys*	
-	1886	0-4-4-0T		1ft 11½in	National Railway Museum, York	*Livingston Thompson*	1
-	1979	0-4-4-0T		1ft 11½in	Ffestiniog Railway	*Earl of Merioneth/ Iarll Meirionnydd*	
-	1992	0-4-4-0T		1ft 11½in	Ffestiniog Railway	12 *David Lloyd George/ Dafydd Lloyd George*	
-	1999	0-4-4T		1ft 11½in	Ffestiniog Railway	*Taliesin*	
14	2010	2-6-2T		1ft 11½in	Ffestiniog Railway	E190 *Lyd*	2

1. On long-term loan from the Ffestiniog Railway. Rebuilt from derelict condition for static display by Winson Engineering, Penrhyndeudraeth in 1988.
2. Construction started by James Evans, Cornwall. A replica of Manning Wardle 2042 of 1925; Lynton & Barnstaple Railway *Lew*.

GARTELL

Gartell Light Railway, Common Lane, Yenston, near Templecombe, Somerset (See also Section 1. British Commercial Locomotive Builders).

Builder's No.	Year	Type	Class	Gauge	Location	Running No./ Name	Notes
-	2008	0-4-0T+T		2ft	Gartell Light Railway	9 *Jean*	

GREAT WESTERN RAILWAY

Swindon Works, Wiltshire.

Builder's No.	Year	Type	Class	Gauge	Location	Running No./ Name	Notes
-	1923	2-6-2T		1ft 11½in	Vale of Rheidol Railway	7 *Owain Glyndŵr*	
-	1923	2-6-2T		1ft 11½in	Vale of Rheidol Railway	8 *Llewellyn*	
-	1924	2-6-2T		1ft 11½in	Vale of Rheidol Railway	9 *Prince of Wales*	1

1. Previously stated elsewhere as built by Davies & Metcalfe in 1902.

LONDON & NORTH WESTERN RAILWAY

Crewe Works, Cheshire.

Builder's No.	Year	Type	Class	Gauge	Location	Running No./ Name	Notes
-	1865	0-4-0ST		1ft 6in	National Railway Museum, York	*Pet*	1

1. Used on Crewe Works internal tramway system until 4/1929, then preserved at the works.

▲ Arn. Jung 4878 of 1930, Mallet-type 0-4-4-0T "Sf. Djatibarang" is a most impressive restoration by the Statfold Barn Railway, as seen on 15 September 2012. **Peter Nicholson**

▼ Henschel 15968 of 1918 is one of several World War I Feldbahn-type 0-8-0Ts imported for preservation. No. 1091 is based on the Toddington Narrow Gauge Railway, and is pictured during celebrations to mark the 50th anniversary of the founding Dowty Railway Preservation Society on 7 October 2012. **Peter Nicholson**

MOORS VALLEY RAILWAY

J. Haylock, Moors Valley Country Park, Horton Road, Ashley Heath, near Ringwood, Dorset.

Builder's No.	Year	Type	Class	Gauge	Location	Running No./ Name	Notes
20	1995	0-4-0T		2ft	Moors Valley Railway	*Emmet*	1

1. Uses the main frame of 0-4-0D Orenstein & Koppel 21160 of 1938. Not operated at MVR (7¼in gauge) but visits other railways. Kept in a container.

NATIONAL MUSEUM OF WALES

Industrial & Maritime Museum, Butetown, Cardiff, South Glamorgan.

Builder's No.	Year	Type	Class	Gauge	Location	Running No./ Name	Notes
-	1981	4wG		4ft 4in	National Waterfront Museum, Swansea		1

1. Working replica of Trevithick 'Penydarren' locomotive of 1804. Overhauled by Ffestiniog Railway, Boston Lodge Works 2014, with new boiler and stronger axles.

F. SAXBY

Normandy near Guildford, Surrey.

Builder's No.	Year	Type	Class	Gauge	Location	Running No./ Name	Notes
1943	1999	4wG		2ft	Frank Saxby, Surrey	*Sue*	1

1. Currently dismantled with parts covered over and not available for viewing.

P. SCOTT

Finnaghy Park Central, Belfast.

Builder's No.	Year	Type	Class	Gauge	Location	Running No./ Name	Notes
-	1969	2-4-0T		1ft 7¼in	Peter Scott, Belfast		1

1. Rebuilt from 2-4-0 in 1970.

TALYLLYN RAILWAY

Pendre Works, Tywyn, Gwynedd.

Builder's No.	Year	Type	Class	Gauge	Location	Running No./ Name	Notes
-	1991	0-4-2T		2ft 3in	Talyllyn Railway	No. 7 *Tom Rolt*	1

1. Built using major components including boiler, wheels and cylinders from ex-Bord na Mona No. LM43 (Barclay 2263 of 1949), a 3ft gauge 0-4-0WT.

4. HOMEBUILT 'COFFEE POT' VERTICAL BOILER LOCOMOTIVES

(See also Section 1 British Commercial Locomotive Builders: de Winton, Keef and Roanoke).

A. C. A. BARBER

North Shropshire & District NG Group, Weston Wharf, Morda.

Builder's No.	Year	Type	Class	Gauge	Location	Running No./ Name	Notes
2	2008	0-4-0TVB		2ft	Oswestry & District Narrow Gauge Group, Weston Wharf, Morda	*Iorwerth*	

A. R. ETHERINGTON

c/o Church Farm, Newbold Verdon, Leicestershire.

Builder's No.	Year	Type	Class	Gauge	Location	Running No./ Name	Notes
-	1969	4wTVBG		2ft	R. P. Morris, Blaenau Ffestiniog	14005 *Steam Tram*	1

1. Uses frame, wheels and gearbox of 4wPM Lister 14005 of 1940.

J. J. FORSHAW

Clifton, Bedfordshire.

Builder's No.	Year	Type	Class	Gauge	Location	Running No./ Name	Notes
-	c1998	4wTVB		2ft	J. J. Forshaw, Clifton, Bedfordshire	*The Iron & Steel Rail Co. Ltd No. 4*	1

1. Currently dismantled for rebuild/overhaul.

A. FOULDS AND R. COLLINS

c/o E. A Foulds Ltd, Albert Works, Clifton Street, Colne, Lancashire.

Builder's No.	Year	Type	Class	Gauge	Location	Running No./ Name	Notes
-	2010	0-4-0TVB		1ft 11½in	Ffestiniog Railway	*Leary*	

T. HALL

North Ings Farm Museum, Fen Road, Dorrington near Ruskington, Lincolnshire LN4 3QB.

Builder's No.	Year	Type	Class	Gauge	Location	Running No./ Name	Notes
1859401	1994	4wTVB		2ft	North Ings Farm Museum	No. 9 *Swift*	1

1. Incorporates major components of *Oddson*, built by J. Marshall 1970.

▲ Krauss 4045 of 1899, 0-4-2T+T "Sragi No. 1" was imported from the Sragi sugar mill, Java and has visited several railways since its restoration at the Statfold Barn Railway. It is pictured at Statfold Barn on 15 September 2012. **Peter Nicholson**

▼ Orenstein & Koppel 614 of 1900, 750mm gauge 0-4-0WT+T Pakis Baru No. 1 was one of the first locomotives to be restored for the dual-gauge, 2ft and 2ft 6in gauge, Statfold Barn Railway. It is seen double-heading with Orenstein & Koppel 1473 of 1905, 0-4-4-0T Mallet Pakis Baru No. 5 on 1 June 2013. **Peter Nicholson**

JAYWICK RAILWAY

Jaywick near Clacton, Essex.

Builder's No.	Year	Type	Class	Gauge	Location	Running No./ Name	Notes
-	1939	(4wTVB)		1ft 6in	Ashover Light Railway project		1

1. Built as a Sentinel-style loco. All that remains are the frame and wheels forming a flat wagon, but it is proposed to rebuild it into a working locomotive again.

C. PARMENTER

c/o Launceston Steam Railway, St Thomas Road, Launceston, Cornwall PL15 8DA.

Builder's No.	Year	Type	Class	Gauge	Location	Running No./ Name	Notes
-	2004–10	2-2-0TVB		600mm	Launceston Steam Railway	*Perseverance*	1

1. Single-cylinder loco built by Christopher Parmenter in LSR workshops 2004. Rebuilt 2009/10 with new main frame.

D. POTTER

Wilbrighton, Shropshire.

Builder's No.	Year	Type	Class	Gauge	Location	Running No./ Name	Notes
2	2008	0-4-0VBG		2ft	Amerton Railway	*Paddy*	1

1. Often visits other railways.

D. C. POTTER

Yaxham Park, Yaxham near Dereham, Norfolk.

Builder's No.	Year	Type	Class	Gauge	Location	Running No./ Name	Notes
-	1970	0-4-0TVBG		2ft	Yaxham Light Railways	No. 1	1

1. Original Merryweather firepump boiler condemned in 1982. To be rebuilt as a steam tram engine.

MR REDSTONE

Penmaenmawr, Caernarvonshire.

Builder's No.	Year	Type	Class	Gauge	Location	Running No./ Name	Notes
-	1905	0-4-0TVB		1ft 11½in	Brecon Mountain Railway		1

1. Built by Mr Redstone, the foreman fitter for the Penmaenmawr Quarries, as a scaled-down copy of a De Winton loco for use on a garden railway operated by quarry owner, C. S. Darbishire. Originally powered on one axle as a 2-2-0; modified to 0-4-0 in the 1920s.

P. S. WEAVER

New Farm, Lacock, Wiltshire.

Builder's No.	Year	Type	Class	Gauge	Location	Running No./ Name	Notes
-	1978	0-4-0TVBG		1ft 9in	P. S. Weaver, Lacock, Wiltshire		1

1. Now stored, out of use.

BUILDER UNKNOWN

Builder's No.	Year	Type	Class	Gauge	Location	Running No./ Name	Notes
-	c1949	(0-4-0TVBG)		2ft	D. Collins, Kanturk, Cork	*(Whistling Willie)*	1

1. Rebuilt as 0-4-0PM and again by Dennis Collins as 4-2-2wPM c2003.

▲ Orenstein & Koppel 10957 of 1925 is one of five 0-10-0Ts imported from Argentina by Preston Services of Canterbury, all of which are awaiting buyers. They are in open-air storage, as seen during a rally event on 28 June 2009.
Cliff Thomas

▲ SLM 924 of 1895, 800mm gauge 0-4-2T Rack loco No. 2 "Enid" is one of eight locomotives supplied to the Snowdon Mountain Railway by SLM. It is seen near the Llanberis terminus on 24 August 2009. Seven of the eight locomotives have survived, the exception being No. 1 "Ladas", which was lost in an accident on the opening day, 6 April 1896. **Peter Nicholson**

▼ Baldwin 44656 of 1917, No. 778 is one of 495 Class 10-12-D 4-6-0Ts supplied to the War Department Light Railways during World War I. It is seen working on the Leighton Buzzard Railway on 8 August 2007, the day of its launch into public service following restoration by the Greensand Railway Museum Trust. **Cliff Thomas**

5. LARGE-SCALE MODEL LOCOMOTIVES

Excludes non-working locomotives built for static display purposes only. The locomotives listed were all built with the capability of being operated in steam, but most are now on static display today.

BAGNALL

W. G. Bagnall Ltd, Castle Engine Works, Stafford, Staffordshire. (See also Section 2 British Commercial Locomotive Builders).

Builder's No.	Year	Type	Class	Gauge	Location	Running No./ Name	Notes
1425	1893	4-2-2		1ft 6in	Preston Services, Canterbury, Kent		1

1. Scale model of a Great Northern Railway Stirling Single.

DAVID CURWEN LTD

Whittonditch, Ramsbury, Marlborough, Wiltshire.

Builder's No.	Year	Type	Class	Gauge	Location	Running No./ Name	Notes
-	1951	4-4-2		1ft 6in	Cleethorpes Coast Light Railway		1

1. Supplied new to Fairy Glen Miniature Railway, New Brighton 4/1951 where named *Crompton*. Fitted with streamlined boiler casing for a period in the 1950s. Stored out of use.

EDINBURGH MUSEUM OF SCIENCE AND ART

Workshop, Chambers Street, Edinburgh, Midlothian.

Builder's No.	Year	Type	Class	Gauge	Location	Running No./ Name	Notes
-	1885	4wG		1ft 7in	National Museum of Scotland, Edinburgh	*Wylam Dilly*	1

1. A 4in-to-1ft scale model of William Hedley locomotive of 1813. On static display.

THOS KENNAN & SON

18-19 Fishamble Street, Dublin.

Builder's No.	Year	Type	Class	Gauge	Location	Running No./ Name	Notes
-	1855	0-6-0		1ft 9in	Trinity College, Dublin		1

1. Scale model of GWR broad gauge 'Pyracmon' class built for instructional purposes. On static display; no tender.

REGENT STREET POLYTECHNIC

Westminster, London W1.

Builder's No.	Year	Type	Class	Gauge	Location	Running No./ Name	Notes
-	1898	4-2-2		1ft 6in	World of Country Life, Exmouth		1

1. Scale model of a Great Northern Railway Stirling Single, built using the design of W. G. Bagnall Ltd, and a boiler and castings supplied by them. On static display.

D. J. SCARROTT

Newton Abbot, Devon.

Builder's No.	Year	Type	Class	Gauge	Location	Running No./ Name	Notes
-	1987	4-6-0		1ft 6in	World of Country Life, Exmouth		1

1. Acquired new and kept on static display.

UNKNOWN

Builder's No.	Year	Type	Class	Gauge	Location	Running No./ Name	Notes
-	c1863	2-2-2		1ft 6in	Unknown, Wiltshire	GNR No. 1	1

1. Previously owned by T. W. Smith, Bitterne, Southampton, Hampshire and before that, by Lord Downshire, Easthampstead, Berkshire.

▲ Baldwin 61269 of 1930, 4-6-2, of typical North American appearance, is a regular performer on the Brecon Mountain Railway, as seen on 17 September 2010. **Cliff Thomas**

6. NEW-BUILD LOCOMOTIVES UNDER CONSTRUCTION

These locos are listed under the organisation which is commissioning the build and which will operate it on completion. Most are being constructed with assistance from other parties, or have been subcontracted to a commercial builder, as detailed.

BEAMISH, THE LIVING MUSEUM OF THE NORTH

Beamish, County Durham DH9 0RG.

Builder's No.	Year	Type	Class	Gauge	Location	Running No./ Name	Notes
BM2	2013–	0-4-0WTG		2ft	Beamish	*Samson*	1

1. The Samson Project – a replica of a locomotive built by Stephen Lewin, Poole Foundry, Dorset in 1874 for the London Lead Co., Cornish Hush Mine, Whitfield Brow, near Frosterley, Co. Durham This was 1ft 10in gauge and believed scrapped c1904. Completion anticipated for early 2015.

BRECON MOUNTAIN RAILWAY

Pant Station, Merthyr Tydfil, Mid Glamorgan CF48 2UP.

Builder's No.	Year	Type	Class	Gauge	Location	Running No./ Name	Notes
		2-6-2		1ft 11¾in	Brecon Mountain Railway	No. 3	1
		2-4-4T	Forney	1ft 11¾in	Brecon Mountain Railway	No. 4	2

1. Being built from original Baldwin Locomotive Works drawings of Sandy River & Rangeley Lakes Railroad (Maine, USA) No. 23 (Baldwin 40733 of 1913).
   A long term-project but many parts have been made and the tender is complete to footplate level. Next, the cylinders will be cast and machined and the main frame erected. The original locomotive weighed 53 tons and was scrapped in 1936 on closure of the railroad.
2. A second locomotive being built from original Baldwin Locomotive Works drawings, of Sandy River & Rangeley Lakes Railroad No. 10 (Baldwin 42231 of 1916).
   Many parts completed with new cylinders being machined in 2014. The original locomotive weighed 33 tons and was also scrapped in 1936.

CORRIS RAILWAY

c/o Alan Keef Ltd, Lea Line, near Ross-on-Wye, Herefordshire HR9 7LQ.

Builder's No.	Year	Type	Class	Gauge	Location	Running No./ Name	Notes
Keef 91		0-4-2ST		2ft 3in	Alan Keef Ltd	No.10	1

1. The Falcon Project – a replica of original Corris Railway locomotive, No. 3 (Hughes 323), now on the Talyllyn Railway (built by Hughes Locomotive & Tramway Engine Works Ltd, Falcon Works, Loughborough as 0-4-0ST in 1878, but later modified to 0-4-2ST).
   Boiler made by Israel Newton in 2012 and the main frames cut by Control Waterjet Cutting, Chesterfield, with assembly of the locomotive being undertaken by Alan Keef Ltd. Completion scheduled by 2015.

▲ Davenport 1586 of 1917, 0-4-0 is one of the more remarkable preservation imports of recent years. It is seen in as-arrived and very poor condition on 1 June 2013, but no doubt it will not be long before it receives the 'Statfold Barn Railway treatment' and is back in service!   **Peter Nicholson**

▼ R. Booth, 1998 0-4-2T "Annie", a replica of Bagnall 1922 of 1911, was built for use on the Groudle Glen Railway, where it is seen on 2 August 2009. It is currently undergoing a rebuild, with replaced items such as cylinders, to be re-used on the North Bay Railway's new-build Bagnall 0-4-0ST "Sipat".   **Peter Nicholson**

GROUDLE GLEN RAILWAY

Lhen Coan, Groudle Glen, Isle of Man.

Builder's No.	Year	Type	Class	Gauge	Location	Running No./ Name	Notes
	2013–	2-4-0T		2ft	Groudle Glen Railway	Brown Bear	1

1. Replica of original GGR *Polar Bear* (Bagnall 1781 of 1905) now at the Amberley Museum. Being assembled in GGR workshops, with a completion target of 2018.

HAYLING SEASIDE RAILWAY

Hayling Island, Hampshire.

Builder's No.	Year	Type	Class	Gauge	Location	Running No./ Name	Notes
		0-4-0	Sweat Pea	2ft	Hayling Seaside Railway		1

1. A scaled-up version of Jack Buckler's 'Sweet Pea' Bagnall-style 0-4-0ST design for 5in gauge. Main frame built with assembly taking place in HSR's workshop.

JOE NEMETH ENGINEERING LTD

Washingpool Farm, Main Road, Easter Compton, Bristol BS35 5RE.

Builder's No.	Year	Type	Class	Gauge	Location	Running No./ Name	Notes
		0-4-0T	Type 1	2ft	Joe Nemeth Engineering		1

1. Replica of a Decauville Type 1 0-4-0T.

LYNTON & BARNSTAPLE RAILWAY

Woody Bay Station, Parracombe, Barnstaple EX31 4RA.

Builder's No.	Year	Type	Class	Gauge	Location	Running No./ Name	Notes
	2009–	2-4-2T		1ft 11½in	Alan Keef Ltd	E762 *Lyn*	1
	2000–	2-6-2T		1ft 11½in	Lynton & Barnstaple Railway	*Yeo*	2

1. The 762 Club is closely linked with the LBR but is a separate company to raise money, build and then maintain and operate a replica of original LBR loco *Lyn* (Baldwin 15965 of 1898; Southern Railway No. E762), which was sold for scrap in 1935.
Assembly is taking place at Alan Keef's works with the main, bar frame to be delivered in late 2014 and a steaming date set for December 2015.
2. A replica of original LBR *Yeo* (Manning Wardle 1361 of 1898; Southern Railway No. E759), which was sold for scrap in 1935. Main frame built by Winson Engineering, Daventry in 2000 and stored at various locations subsequently, and now on display at LBR, Woody Bay.

NORTH BAY RAILWAY

Burniston Road, Scarborough, North Yorkshire YO12 6PF.

Builder's No.	Year	Type	Class	Gauge	Location	Running No./ Name	Notes
	2013–	0-4-0ST	Sipat	1ft 8in	North Bay Railway	Georgina	1
	2014–	0-4-0ST	Sipat	2ft	North Bay Railway		1

1. Replica of 2ft gauge Bagnall 0-4-0ST 'Sipat' class of 1908 being built in the NBR workshops by North Bay Railway Engineering Services Ltd. The original *Sipat* was Bagnall 1868 of 1908. The first loco due to be completed in 2014. The second loco will visit other railways.

SOUTHWOLD RAILWAY

Southwold Railway Trust, Southwold, Suffolk.

Builder's No.	Year	Type	Class	Gauge	Location	Running No./ Name	Notes
	2010–	2-4-0T		3ft	Southwold Railway project	No. 3 *Blyth*	1

1. Replica of original Southwold Railway locomotive (Sharp Stewart 2850 of 1879), scrapped in 1941. Being built in the SRT's workshops, by the 2-4-0 Club, but may be completed elsewhere.

STATION ROAD STEAM/JAMES WATERFIELD

Unit 16-17 Moorlands Industrial Estate, Metheringham, Lincolnshire, LN4 3HX.

Builder's No.	Year	Type	Class	Gauge	Location	Running No./ Name	Notes
	2013–	0-4-0ST	Sipat	2ft	Station Road Steam		1
	2013–	0-4-0ST	Sipat	2ft	Station Road Steam		1
	2013–	0-4-0ST	Sipat	2ft	Station Road Steam		1

1. A batch of three locomotives being built to the design of Bagnall 'Sipat' class of 1908. Original *Sipat* was Bagnall 1868 of 1908.

J. UPHILL

c/o Gartell Light Railway, Common Lane, Yenston, near Templecombe, Somerset, and c/o Lynton & Barnstaple Railway, Woody Bay, Parracombe, Devon EX314RA.

Builder's No.	Year	Type	Class	Gauge	Location	Running No./ Name	Notes
		0-4-0			Gartell Light Railway		1

1. Construction started in Gartell Light Railway's workshops; components to be moved to Lynton & Barnstaple Railway Woody Bay 2014 for completion by John Uphill.

WELSH HIGHLAND HERITAGE RAILWAY

Gelert's Farm, Porthmadog.

Builder's No.	Year	Type	Class	Gauge	Location	Running No./ Name	Notes
	2006–	0-4-0ST		1ft 11½in	Welsh Highland Heritage Railway	*Lady Madcap*	1

1. A re-creation of Dinorwic Quarries Hunslet 652 of 1896 by a group of WHHR members using a new main frame with many original parts from this and other quarry Hunslets. The original locomotive withdrawn in 1952 and scrapped in 1969.

▲▼ Festiniog Railway 14 of 2010, 2-6-2T No. E190 "Lyd" was a long-term build recreating the long-lost Lynton & Barnstaple loco "Lew". It made a triumphant visit to the new Lynton & Barnstaple Railway at Woody Bay for the May 2013 gala. **Peter Nicholson**

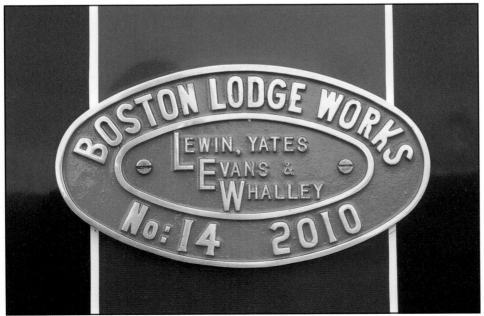

▲ Festiniog 1879, 0-4-4-0 double Fairlie, No. 10 "Merddin Emrys" is seen on The Cob, approaching Porthmadog Harbour station on 4 May 2013. **Cliff Thomas**

▼ Gartell, 2008. 0-4-0T+T No. 9 "Jean", construction of which was started at home by Dr Alan White and completed in the Gartell railway's workshops, runs around its train at Tower View on 7 May 2012. This was the opening day of the station and extension on the old Somerset & Dorset Joint Railway trackbed. **Peter Nicholson**

APPENDIX I. INDEX OF LOCOMOTIVE NAMES

Name	Builder	Builder's Section No.	
Holy War	Hunslet	779	(1.)
Hugh Napier	Hunslet	855	(1.)
Hutchinson	Beyer Peacock	5126	(1.)
Iarll Meirionnydd	Festiniog Railway	-	(3.)
Iorwerth	A. C. A. Barber	-	(4.)
Irish Mail	Hunslet	823	(1.)
Isaac	Bagnall	3023	(1.)
Isabel	Bagnall	1491	(1.)
Isibutu	Bagnall	2820	(1.)
Jack	Barclay	1871	(1.)
Jack	Hunslet	684	(1.)
Jack Lane	Hunslet (Statfold)	3904	(1.)
Janice	North British	27291	(1.)
Jean	Gartell	-	(3.)
Jennie	Hunslet (Statfold)	3905	(1.)
Jenny	Arn. Jung	3175	(2.)
Jerry M.	Hunslet	638	(1.)
Joan	Kerr Stuart	4404	(1.)
Joan	T. D. A. Civil	1	(3.)
Joffre	Kerr Stuart	2405	(1.)
Jonathan	Hunslet	678	(1.)
Josephine	Hunslet	1842	(1.)
Jubilee 1897	Manning Wardle	1382	(1.)
Jurassic	Peckett	1008	(1.)
Justine	Arn. Jung	939	(2.)
Kanaka	Hudswell, Clarke	1056	(1.)
Karen	Peckett	2024	(1.)
Kathleen	De Winton	-	(1.)
(Kathleen)	Robert Stephenson	2613	(1.)
Katie	Arn. Jung	3872	(2.)
Kettering Furnaces No. 3	Beyer Peacock	859	(1.)
Kettering Furnaces No. 8	Manning Wardle	1675	(1.)
Kidbrooke	Bagnall	2043	(1.)
King of the Scarlets	Hunslet	492	(1.)
Kissack	Beyer Peacock	5382	(1.)
Lady Joan	Hunslet	1429	(1.)
Lady Madcap	Welsh Highland Heritage Railway	-	(6.)
La Herrera	Sabero	-	(2.)
Leader	Kerr Stuart	926	(1.)
Leary	A. Foulds & R. Collins	-	(4.)
Lee Moor No. 1	Peckett	783	(1.)
Lee Moor No. 2	Peckett	784	(1.)
Lena	Kerr Stuart	1098	(1.)
Leonard	Bagnall	2087	(1.)
Liassic	Peckett	1632	(1.)
Lilian	Hunslet	317	(1.)
Lilla	Hunslet	554	(1.)
Limpopo	Fowler	18800	(1.)
Linda	Hunslet	590	(1.)
Lisboa	Falcon	266	(1.)
Livingston Thompson	Festiniog Railway	-	(3.)
Llanfair	De Winton	-	(1.)
Llewellyn	Great Western Railway	-	(3.)
Loch	Beyer Peacock	1416	(1.)
Lord Granby	Hudswell, Clarke	633	(1.)
Lorna Doone	Kerr Stuart	4250	(1.)
Lucy	Kerr Stuart	1313	(1.)
Lyd	Festiniog Railway	14	(3.)
Lyn	Lynton & Barnstaple Railway 762 Club	-	(6.)
Maid Marian	Hunslet	822	(1.)
Maitland	Beyer Peacock	4663	(1.)
Mannin	Beyer Peacock	6296	(1.)
Marchlyn	Avonside	2067	(1.)
Margaret	Hunslet	605	(1.)
Matheran	Orenstein & Koppel	2343	(2.)
Meenglass	Nasmyth, Wilson	828	(1.)
Melior	Kerr Stuart	4219	(1.)
Merddin Emrys	Festiniog Railway	-	(3.)
Merlen Gymreig	England	234	(1.)
Mesozoic	Peckett	1327	(1.)
Michael	Hunslet	1709	(1.)
Millennium/ Mileniwm	Beyer Peacock	7863	(1.)
Mines de Aller 2	Corpet Louvet	439	(2.)
Moel Siabod	SLM	989	(2.)
(Mona)	Beyer Peacock	1417	(1.)
Monarch	Bagnall	3024	(1.)
Montalban	Orenstein & Koppel	6641	(2.)
Mountaineer	Alco	57156	(2.)
Mr. G	North Dorset	698	(1.)
Naklo	Fablok (Chrzanow)	3459	(2.)
Nancy	Avonside	1547	(1.)
Nutty	Sentinel	7701	(1.)
Ogwen	Avonside	2066	(1.)
Olleros	Couillet	1318	(2.)
Owain Glyndŵr	Great Western Railway	-	(3.)
Padarn	SLM	2838	(2.)
Paddy	D. Potter	2	(4.)
Palmerston	England	-	(1.)
Pamela	Hunslet	920	(1.)
P. C. Allen	Orenstein & Koppel	5834	(2.)
Pedemoura	Orenstein & Koppel	10808	(2.)
Pender	Beyer Peacock	1255	(1.)
Pendyffryn	De Winton	-	(1.)
Penlee	Freudenstein	73	(2.)
(Penmaen)	De Winton	-	(1.)
Perseverance	C. Parmenter	-	(4.)
Pet	London & North Western Railway	-	(3.)
Peter	Bagnall	2067	(1.)
Peter Pan	Kerr Stuart	4256	(1.)
Peveril	Beyer Peacock	1524	(1.)
Phoenix	Atkinson Walker	114	(1.)
Phoenix	Ferndale	21	(2.)
Pixie	Bagnall	2090	(1.)
Pixie	Kerr Stuart	4260	(1.)

▲ Great Western Railway 1924, 2-6-2T No. 9 "Prince of Wales", built at Swindon Works for the Vale of Rheidol Railway, made its debut in newly applied Cambrian Railways livery on 27 May 2014. This livery has been applied to mark the 150th anniversary of the Cambrian Railways company. **Cliff Thomas**

▼ Moors Valley Railway 20 of 1995, 0-4-0T "Emmet" is kept in the 7¼in gauge MVR station when not visiting other railways. Builder and MVR operator Jim Haylock is at the controls on a visit to the Purbeck Mineral & Mining Museum, Norden, Dorset on 6 September 2013. An appropriate location as the diesel locomotive whose frame was used in this loco used to work on the clay mine lines here. **Peter Nicholson**

Name	Builder	Builder's Section No.		Name	Builder	Builder's Section No.	
Polar Bear	Bagnall	1781	(1.)	Sutherland	Beyer Peacock	1263	(1.)
Premier	Kerr Stuart	886	(1.)	Sybil	Bagnall	1760	(1.)
Prince	England	-	(1.)	Sybil	Hunslet	827	(1.)
Prince of Wales	Great Western			Sybil Mary	Hunslet	921	(1.)
	Railway	-	(3.)	Swift	T. Hall	1859401	
Princess	England	200	(1.)				(4.)
Ralph	SLM	2869	(2.)	Taffy	Keef	30	(1.)
Rebecca	Orenstein &			Taliesin	Festiniog Railway	-	(3.)
	Koppel	5744	(2.)	Talyllyn	Fletcher Jennings	42	(1.)
Renishaw 4	Avonside	2057	(1.)	The Coalition	Bagnall	1278	(1.)
Renishaw 5	Bagnall	2545	(1.)	The Earl	Beyer Peacock	3496	(1.)
Rheneas	Fletcher Jennings	63	(1.)	The Eclipse	Bagnall	1445	(1.)
Rishra	Baguley	2007	(1.)	The Iron & Steel			
Rough Pup	Hunslet	541	(1.)	Rail Co. Ltd			
Rur	Henschel	5276	(2.)	No. 4	J. J. Forshaw	-	(4.)
Russell	Hunslet	901	(1.)	Thomas Bach	Hunslet	849	(1.)
Sabero	Couillet	1140	(2.)	Thomas			
Saccharine	Fowler	13355	(1.)	Edmondson	Henschel	16047	(2.)
Samelices	Couillet	1209	(2.)	Thomas			
Samson	Beamish	BM2	(6.)	Wicksteed	Hunslet (Statfold)	3906	(1.)
San Justo	Hudswell, Clarke	639	(1.)	Thornhill	Beyer Peacock	2028	(1.)
Santa Ana	Hudswell, Clarke	640	(1.)	Tjepper	Arn. Jung	2279	(2.)
Santa Teresa	Baldwin	15515	(2.)	Tom Rolt	Barclay/		
Sao Domingos	Orenstein &				Talyllyn Railway	2263	(1.)
	Koppel	11784	(2.)	Tourska	Fablok		
Scaldwell	Peckett	1316	(1.)		(Chrzanow)	3512	(2.)
Sea Lion	Bagnall	1484	(1.)	Townsend Hook	Fletcher Jennings	172L	(1.)
(Secundus)	Bellis & Seekings	-	(1.)	Trangkil No. 4	Hunslet	3902	(1.)
Sezela No. 2	Avonside	1720	(1.)	Triassic	Peckett	1270	(1.)
Sezela No. 4	Avonside	1738	(1.)	Triumph	Bagnall	2511	(1.)
Sezela No. 6	Avonside	1928	(1.)	Tynwald	Beyer Peacock	2038	(1.)
Sgt Murphy	Kerr Stuart	3117	(1.)	Tyrone	Peckett	1026	(1.)
Shane	Barclay	2265	(1.)	Una	Hunslet	873	(1.)
Siam	Henschel	29582	(2.)	Unique	Bagnall	2216	(1.)
Sinembe	Bagnall	2287	(1.)	Utrillas	Orenstein &		
Sir Drefaldwyn	Franco-Belge	2855	(2.)		Koppel	2378	(2.)
Sir Handel	Hughes	323	(1.)	Velinheli	Hunslet	409	(1.)
Sir Haydn	Hughes	323	(1.)	Veracruz	Orenstein &		
(Sir Neville					Koppel	11009	(2.)
Lubbock)	Kerr Stuart	857/858?	(1.)	Victory	Decauville	246	(2.)
Sir Tom	Bagnall	2135	(1.)	(Watkin)	De Winton	-	(1.)
Skarloey	Fletcher Jennings	42	(1.)	Welsh Pony	England	234	(1.)
Slieve Callan	Dübs	2890	(1.)	Wendy	Bagnall	2091	(1.)
Snowdon	SLM	988	(2.)	(Whistling Willie)	Unknown	-	(4.)
Sotillos	Borsig	6022	(2.)	Wild Aster	Hunslet	849	(1.)
(Springbok)	Beyer Peacock	7827	(1.)	William Finlay	Fletcher Jennings	173L	(1.)
Sragi No. 1	Krauss	4045	(2.)	Winifred	Hunslet	364	(1.)
Sragi 14 Max	Orenstein &			Woolwich	Avonside	1748	(1.)
	Koppel	10750	(2.)	Woto	Bagnall	2133	(1.)
St. Djatibarang	Arn. Jung	4878	(2.)	Wren	Beyer Peacock	2825	(1.)
Stanhope	Kerr Stuart	2395	(1.)	Wyddfa	SLM	925	(2.)
Statfold	Hunslet (Statfold)	3903	(1.)	Wylam Dilly	Edinburgh		
Steam Tram	A. R. Etherington	-	(4.)		Museum	-	(5.)
Sue	F. Saxby	1943	(3.)	Yeo	Lynton &		
Superb	Bagnall	2624	(1.)		Barnstaple		
Superior	Kerr Stuart	4034	(1.)		Railway	-	(6.)
Susan	Orenstein &			Zambezi	Fowler	13573	(1.)
	Koppel	3136	(2.)				

APPENDIX II. LIST OF LOCATIONS

The following are the railways and other locations where narrow gauge steam locomotives can be seen by members of the public, at least on occasions. Opening and operating times need to be checked before making a visit. While some railways operate a regular steam-hauled service others may only have steam in operation on special weekends. These can be visiting locomotives so they do not necessarily have such engines available at other times, but all sites listed have at least one locomotive in residence, even if currently out of traffic.

Unless special prior arrangement is made it is almost certain that some locomotives will not be available for viewing during a visit. These are perhaps dismantled for repair and overhaul in a workshop, kept in a locked shed not being in use that day, or are being kept out of sight under covers, awaiting attention.

Many narrow gauge steam locomotives are in private ownership, some operated on extensive private railways and are unfortunately not readily accessible to the public. These are shown in the loco list with the owner's name and nearest town or county. Only those sites with regular steam operations, open days or a steam loco on site and open to the public at least one day a year are included in the list below.

Many of these railways only run a public service on certain days, such as Sundays and Bank Holidays Mondays, say April to September and are only accessible on those days. Others run similarly, but being part of a larger attraction which is open more often, much of the stock can be seen at other times, albeit statically. Sites which are private, and only open to the public on a few days each year are marked*.

The address given is the main point of access to the site and is not necessarily where the locomotives are kept, this sometimes being well away from the entrance.

HERITAGE RAILWAYS, MUSEUMS & COLLECTIONS

	OS GRD REF.
Abbey Pumping Station, Corporation Road, off Abbey Lane, Leicester.	SK 589067
Alan Keef Ltd, Lea Line, near Ross-on-Wye, Herefordshire.*	SO 665214
Amberley Museum, Houghton Bridge, Amberley, West Sussex.	TQ 031122
Amerton Railway, Amerton Farm, Stowe-by-Chartley, Stafford.	SJ 993278
Apedale Valley Light Railway, Apedale Community Park, Chesterton, Staffordshire.	SJ 823484
Bala Lake Railway, Llanuwchllyn, near Bala, Gwynedd.	SH 881300
Beamish, The Living Museum of the North, Beamish, Co. Durham.	NZ 214548
Brecon Mountain Railway, Pant Station, Merthyr Tydfil, Mid Glamorgan.	SO 060098
and museum at Pontsticill Station.	SO 063120
Bredgar & Wormshill Light Railway, The Warren, Bredgar, Sittingbourne, Kent.	TQ 873585
Bressingham Steam and Gardens, Low Road, Bressingham, near Diss, Norfolk.	TM 080806
Buckinghamshire Railway Centre, Quainton Road Station, Buckinghamshire.	
Bursledon Light Railway (Hampshire Narrow Gauge Railway Trust),	
Bursledon Brickworks, 148 Swanwick Lane, Lower Swanwick, Hampshire.	SU 499098
Cavan & Leitrim Railway, Dromod Station, Dromod, Co. Leitrim –	
see also Irish Narrow Gauge Trust	
Cleethorpes Coast Light Railway, Kings Road, Cleethorpes, Lincolnshire.	TA 321073
Corris Railway, Station Yard, Corris, Gwynedd.	SH 755078
Devon Railway Centre, Cadleigh Station, Bickleigh, near Tiverton, Devon.	SS 938076
Eastwell History Group, Eastwell, Leicestershire.	
Engine House, The Severn Valley Railway, Highley, Shropshire.	SO 749831
Exmoor Steam Railway, Bratton Fleming, Devon – now a private site not open to	
the public.	
Ffestiniog Railway, Porthmadog (to Blaenau Ffestiniog), Gwynedd.	
Foyle Valley Railway Museum, Londonderry, Co. Derry.	
Gartell Light Railway, Common Lane, Yenston, near Templecombe, Somerset.*	ST 718218
Giant's Causeway & Bushmills Railway, near Bushmills, Co. Antrim.	C 943437
Golden Valley Light Railway, Midland Railway-Butterley, Swanwick Junction,	
Derbyshire.	SK 412519
Great Bush Railway, Tinkers Park, Hadlow Down, East Sussex*	TQ 538241

Great Laxey Mine Railway, Valley Gardens, Laxey, Isle of Man.	SC 433847
Great Whipsnade Railway, Whipsnade Zoo, Bedfordshire.	TL 004172
Groudle Glen Railway, Lhen Coan, Groudle Glen, Isle of Man.	SC 418786
Guinness Storehouse, St James's Gate Brewery, Crane Street, Dublin 8.	
Hampshire Narrow Gauge Railway Trust – see Bursledon Light Railway.	
Hampton & Kempton Waterworks Railway, Kempton Park Water Treatment Works, Snakey Lane, Hanworth, Middlesex.	TQ 111708
Hayling Seaside Railway, Hayling Island, Hampshire	
Hollycombe Working Steam Museum, Iron Hill, Liphook, West Sussex.	SU 852295
Hull Streetlife Museum of Transport, High Street, Kingston upon Hull, East Yorkshire.	TA 103287
Irchester Narrow Gauge Railway Museum, Irchester Country Park, Wellingborough, Northamptonshire.	SP 906660
Irish Narrow Gauge Trust, Dromod Station, Dromod, Co. Leitrim – see also Cavan & Leitrim Railway.	
Irish Steam Preservation Society, Stradbally Hall, Stradbally Co. Laois.	S 568966
Ironbridge Gorge Museum, Blists Hill Victorian Town, Madeley, Telford, Shropshire.	SJ 693033
Isle of Man Steam Railway, Douglas (to Port Erin), Isle of Man.	SC 377753
Launceston Steam Railway, Newport Industrial Estate, Launceston, Cornwall.	SX 328850
Leadhills & Wanlockhead Railway, Leadhills, South Lanarkshire.	NS 888145
Leeds Industrial Museum, Armley Mills, Canal Road, Leeds, West Yorkshire.	SE 275342
Leighton Buzzard Railway, Page's Park, Leighton Buzzard, Bedfordshire.	SP 928242
Lincolnshire Coast Light Railway, Skegness Water Leisure Park, Walls Lane, Ingoldmells, Skegness, Lincolnshire.	TF 562671
Llanberis Lake Railway, Gilfach Ddu, Llanberis, Gwynedd.	SH 586603
Locomotion – The National Railway Museum at Shildon, Co. Durham.	NZ 240255
London Museum of Water & Steam (formerly Kew Bridge Steam Museum), Green Dragon Lane, Brentford, Gr London.	TQ 188780
Lynton & Barnstaple Railway, Woody Bay Station, near Parracombe, Devon.	SS 682464
Mizens Railway (7¼in gauge), Barrs Lane, Knaphill, Woking, Surrey.	SU 967593
Moseley Railway Trust – see Apedale Valley Light Railway.	
Museum of Science & Industry (MOSI), Liverpool Road, Castlefield, Manchester.	SJ 831978
Narrow Gauge Railway Museum, Talyllyn Railway, Wharf Station, Tywyn, Gwynedd.	SH 586004
National Museum of Scotland, Chambers Street, Edinburgh.	NT 258734
National Railway Museum, Leeman Road, York, North Yorkshire.	SE 594519
National Trust, Industrial Railway Museum, Penrhyn Castle near Bangor, Gwynedd.	SH 603720
National Waterfront Museum, Oystermouth Road, Maritime Quarter, Swansea.	SS 659927
North Bay Railway, Northstead Manor Gardens, Burniston Road, North Bay, Scarborough, North Yorkshire.	TA 035898
North Ings Farm Museum, Fen Road, Dorrington, near Ruskington, Lincolnshire.*	TF 098527
Old Kiln Light Railway, The Rural Life Centre, Reeds Road, Tilford, Surrey.	SU 858434
Port Erin Railway Museum (Isle of Man Railway), Port Erin, Isle of Man.	SC 198689
Preston Services, Preston, near Canterbury, Kent.*	TR 244604
Purbeck Mineral & Mining Museum, Nordern Park & Ride, near Corfe Castle, Dorset.	SZ 957829
Railway Preservation Society of Ireland (RPSI), Whitehead Depot, Co. Antrim.	J 474922
Ravenglass & Eskdale Railway, Ravenglass, Cumbria.	SD 086964
Riverside Museum, 100 Pointhouse Place, Glasgow.	
Scottish Railway Preservation Society, Union Street, Bo'ness, West Lothian.	NT 003817
Sittingbourne & Kemsley Light Railway, Sittingbourne, Kent.	TQ 904642
Snowdon Mountain Railway, Llanberis, Gwynedd.	SH582597
South Devon Railway, Lee Moor Tramway Museum, Buckfastleigh, Devon.	SX 747663
South Tynedale Railway, Alston, Cumbria.	NY 717467
Statfold Barn Railway, Ashby Road, Tamworth, Staffordshire.*	SK 241064
Stradbally Steam Museum, Main Street, The Green, Stradbally, Co. Laois.	S 575961
Strumpshaw Steam Museum, Old Hall, Strumpshaw, near Acle, Norfolk.	TG 345065
Summerlee, Museum of Scottish Industrial Life, Heritage Way, Coatbridge, North Lanarkshire.	NS 728655
Swanage Railway, Corfe Castle Station, Dorset.	
Talyllyn Railway, Tywyn, Gwynedd.	SH590008
Tanfield Railway, Marley Hill, Co. Durham.	NZ 207573
Teifi Valley Railway, Henllan, near Llandysul, Ceredigion (not currently operational).	SN 357406
Telford Horsehay Steam Trust, The Old Loco Shed, Bridge Road, Horsehay, Telford, Shropshire.	SJ 675073
Threlkeld Quarry & Mining Museum, Threlkeld Quarry, near Keswick, Cumbria.	NY 320245
Thursford Collection, Thursford, near Fakenham, Norfolk.	TF 980345

Toddington Narrow Gauge Railway, Gloucestershire Warwickshire Railway,
    Toddington Station, Gloucestershire.   SP 048318
Tralee & Dingle Steam Railway, Blennerville, near Tralee, Co. Kerry.
Ulster Folk & Transport Museum, Cultra, Holywood, Co. Down.   J 419806
Vale of Rheidol Railway, Aberystwyth (to Devil's Bridge), Ceredigion.   SN 587812
Vale of Rheidol Railway, Surrey – private site; locomotives stored with those of
    P. Rampton.
Welsh Highland Heritage Railway, Porthmadog, Gwynedd .   SH 571393
Welsh Highland Railway, Dinas, (Caernarfon to Porthmadog), Gwynedd.   SH 477587
Welshpool & Llanfair Light Railway, Llanfair Caereinon (to Welshpool), Powys.   SJ 107069
Welsh Slate Museum, Gilfach Ddu, Llanberis, Gwynedd.
West Lancashire Light Railway, Station Road, Hesketh Bank, Lancashire.   SD448229
Wheal Martyn, Carthew, St Austell, Cornwall.   SX 004555
World of Country Life, Sandy Bay, Exmouth, Devon.   SY 035808
Yaxham Light Railways, Yaxham, near Dereham, Norfolk.*   TG 003102

▲ D. Potter 2 of 2008, 0-4-0VBG, "Paddy", built by David Potter and friends is based at the Amerton
Railway, but has visited many railways, including Alan Keef's open day, on 22 September 2012.
Unusually for a 'coffee pot' locomotive, it has a tender.   **Peter Nicholson**

PLATFORM 5 MAIL ORDER

TRACKatlas

of Mainland Britain 2nd edition

The much anticipated second edition of TRACKatlas of Mainland Britain, published by Platform 5. As well as being completely revised and updated, this new volume has been further enhanced by the inclusion of 44 major heritage railways, including several narrow gauge lines. A greater number of locations now benefit from inset maps and the London inset maps have all been redrawn to provide greater clarity and a consistent scale throughout. Much work has been undertaken to provide additional detail across the network, the extent being too exhaustive to list here in full. Now includes 139 detailed map pages.

- All passenger and freight routes are shown with their track formations including connections, crossovers and primary sidings.
- All stations are shown with platform detail and with railway mileages denoted in miles and chains.
- Most signal boxes, junctions and tunnels are shown including their names and railway mileages.
- Most level crossings are included together with information describing their type.
- Complex areas are shown as larger scale insets.
- Different colours are used to denote electrification type and voltage.
- A comprehensive index contains over 9000 entries.

176 pages. A4 size. Hardback. Published 2012. £24.95.

HOW TO ORDER

Telephone your order and credit/debit card details to our 24-hour sales orderline:

0114 255 8000 or Fax: 0114 255 2471. An answerphone is attached for calls made outside of normal UK office hours. Or send your credit/debit card details, sterling cheque, money order or British Postal order payable to 'Platform 5 Publishing Ltd.' to:

Mail Order Department (NGSL), Platform 5 Publishing Ltd, 52 Broadfield Road, SHEFFIELD, S8 0XJ, ENGLAND.

Please add postage & packing: 10% UK; 20% Europe; 30% Rest of World. Please allow 28 days for delivery in the UK.